info@kinfolk.com
www.kinfolk.com

Kinfolk Magazine
328 NE Failing Street
Portland, Oregon 97212
Telephone: 503-946-8400

Printed in Canada

Publication Design by Amanda Jane Jones
Cover Photograph by Charlie Schuck

KINFOLK

NATHAN WILLIAMS
EDITOR IN CHIEF & CREATIVE DIRECTOR

GEORGIA FRANCES KING
EDITOR

GAIL O'HARA
MANAGING EDITOR

ANJA VERDUGO
ART DIRECTOR

AMANDA JANE JONES
LEAD DESIGNER

JENNIFER JAMES WRIGHT
DESIGNER

DOUG BISCHOFF
BUSINESS OPERATIONS

KATIE SEARLE-WILLIAMS
BUSINESS MANAGER

PAIGE BISCHOFF
ACCOUNTS PAYABLE & RECEIVABLE

JULIE POINTER
COMMUNITY DIRECTOR

JESSICA GRAY
STUDIO MANAGER

NATHAN TICKNOR
SERVICE MANAGER

JOANNA HAN
CONTRIBUTING EDITOR

ERIC DAVIS
WEB ADMINISTRATOR

KELSEY B. SNELL
PROOFREADER

KELSEY VALA
EDITORIAL ASSISTANT & RECIPE EDITOR

HANNAH MENDENHALL
EDITORIAL ASSISTANT & PHOTOGRAPHER

MEREDITH MCENTEE
EDITORIAL ASSISTANT

JACOB SEARLE
EDITORIAL ASSISTANT

SUBSCRIBE

Kinfolk is published four times a year.
To subscribe, visit *www.kinfolk.com/shop*
or email us at *subscribe@kinfolk.com*

CONTACT US

If you have questions or comments,
write to us at *info@kinfolk.com*

WWW.KINFOLK.COM

WELCOME

"The sea, once it casts its spell, holds one in its net of wonder forever"

—JACQUES-YVES COUSTEAU

No summer would be complete without salt. We are more connected to both the sea and seasoning than you might think, which is probably why the rising temperature brings with it an urge to seek the closest body of water and dive in headfirst. The lingering hint of salt that rests on your lips after a day by the ocean is a sign of a well-spent summer, and in this issue we'd like to suggest a few more ways to enjoy those sun-soaked days.

The Saltwater Issue of *Kinfolk* is a double-barreled exploration into the world's most ubiquitous mineral that also doubles as one of the season's key ingredients. Our summer edition will look at it in its cultural context, the coastal waters it bathes in and the kinds of people who frolic in its watery habitat (plus suggestions for how you can join them). Think of it as a carefree summer issue seasoned with a pinch of culinary history.

There are essays on squid and Steinbeck, recipes for snow cones and fish tacos, and illustrated guides to summer jobs and sailor tattoos. Our list for getting optimal Vitamin D without second-degree burns will save your skin, the regular How To Be Neighborly column gets a witty update for its beach towel edition and we put the word out to some food experts to tell us what's what in the modern salt landscape. We also took a visual trip to South America to visit two countries with particularly salty terrains: Bolivia's Salar de Uyuni, the largest salt desert in the world, spanning more than 4,000 square miles, and Peru's Salinas de Maras, which contains hundreds of salt evaporation ponds that date back to pre-Inca times.

One artist shares his work made using only a rake and the California coastline as a canvas, and in case you'd like to make a seriously fancy beach sculpture of your own, we asked one of the world's best sandcastle makers to share some tips. This issue would not be complete without interviewing the mighty Marks of salt: Both Bitterman and Kurlansky's tomes on the subject have brought more awareness to the seasoning. We spoke to them about their lives inside and outside the kitchen. Other interviews include a communal reflection from marine biologists and water dwellers on the changing state of the sea, plus an insight into an innovative salt maker who evaporates seawater 17 stories above the streets of Manhattan.

In the end, we encourage you to walk—or swim—away from this issue with the inclination to get outside and revel in the tastes and feelings of summer. Come on in: The water's warm.

NATHAN WILLIAMS AND GEORGIA FRANCES KING

ANAÏS & DAX
Photographers
New York, New York

ANDRES AMADOR
Artist
San Francisco, California

ROMY ASH
Writer
Melbourne, Australia

CHRISTOPHER BARSCH
Food Stylist
Brooklyn, New York

MARCUS MØLLER BITSCH
Photographer
Aarhus, Denmark

KAYE BLEGVAD
Illustrator
New York, New York

JAMES BOWDEN
Photographer
Bournemouth, United Kingdom

SARAH BURWASH
Illustrator
Nova Scotia, Canada

JAMES CHOROROS
Photographer
New York, New York

KATRIN COETZER
Illustrator
Cape Town, South Africa

DAVID COGGINS
Writer
New York, New York

JOSEPH CONWAY
Photographer
Brighton, United Kingdom

KIRA CORBIN
Prop Stylist
Brooklyn, New York

CARLY DIAZ
Writer
Portland, Oregon

SCARLETT HOOFT GRAAFLAND
Photographer
Amsterdam, the Netherlands

KATE S. JORDAN
Prop Stylist
Pound Ridge, New York

KATE MAYES
Writer
Sydney, Australia

ANNE PARKER
Stylist
Portland, Oregon

NIKAELA MARIE PETERS
Writer
Winnipeg, Canada

CHARLIE SCHUCK
Photographer
Seattle, Washington

AGNES THOR
Photographer
New York, New York

THE WEAVER HOUSE
Photographers
Portland, Oregon

DANIEL CROCKETT
Writer
La Galaube, France

TRAVIS ELBOROUGH
Writer
London, United Kingdom

ASHLEY HELVEY
Stylist
Seattle, Washington

KATHRIN KOSCHITZKI
Photographer
Nuremberg, Germany

REBECCA MICCICHE
Stylist
Portland, Oregon

NIRAV PATEL
Photographer
San Francisco, California

RICKY PIÑA
Writer
Los Angeles, California

SHANTANU STARICK
Photographer
Brisbane, Australia

NICOLE VILLENEUVE
Writer
New York, New York

WICHMANN + BENDTSEN
Photographers
Copenhagen, Denmark

RYAN DAUSCH
Photographer
Brooklyn, New York

ALICE GAO
Photographer
New York, New York

WILLIAM HEREFORD
Photographer
Brooklyn, New York

LINDSAY LARICKS
Writer
Kansas City, Missouri

BOBBY MILLS
Photographer
Brighton, United Kingdom

TEC PETAJA
Photographer
Nashville, Tennessee

MARK SANDERS
Photographer
London, United Kingdom

KATIE STRATTON
Painter
Dayton, Ohio

HELLE WALSTED
Stylist
Copenhagen, Denmark

DIANA YEN
Writer & Food Stylist
New York, New York

ONE

4

MASTHEAD

5

WELCOME

6

KINFOLK COMMUNITY

14

THE SALINE SOLUTION: AN ESSAY LOOKING
INTO OUR SIMILARITIES TO THE SEA

Daniel Crockett

16

ROLLING IN THE DEEP: AN ESSAY ABOUT
THE POETRY IN WHALE SONGS

Nikaela Marie Peters

18

ONE LAZY SUMMER: A PHOTO ESSAY
TO INSPIRE THAT SUMMER FEELING

Agnes Thor

24

WRITING THE WAVES: AN EXPLORATION INTO HOW
JOHN STEINBECK FOUND A MUSE IN THE SEA

Nicole Villeneuve

26

HOW TO BE NEIGHBORLY: AN ILLUSTRATED GUIDE
TO KEEPING THE PEACE IN TOWEL TERRITORY

Georgia Frances King

32

THE ONE THAT GOT AWAY: A FAILED FISHERMAN'S
GUIDE TO (NOT) CATCHING THINGS

David Coggins

34

SWIMMING WITH SHARKS: AN ESSAY ABOUT
OVERCOMING OUR FEARS OF THE OCEAN

Kate Mayes

36

SALT AND VINEGAR MENU: A SERIES OF
RECIPES INSPIRED BY THE CLASSIC PAIRING

Diana Yen

38

SALT AND VINEGAR MENU: STUFFED
SALT AND VINEGAR POTATO SKINS

Diana Yen

40

SALT AND VINEGAR MENU: GRILLED CHICKEN
WITH BLACKBERRY BALSAMIC SAUCE

Diana Yen

42

BRITISH BEACH TOWNS: A LIST OF ESSENTIAL
ELEMENTS FOR SEASIDE VILLAGES

Travis Elborough

44

TAFFY TALES: A LOOK INTO THE STORY
BEHIND SALT WATER TAFFY

Carly Diaz

TWO

48

THE LINGERING SALT OF SWEAT: A SERIES
OF SWELTERING PORTRAITS

Charlie Schuck

56

A LETTER FROM PEPPER: A REBUTTAL
FROM THE NEGLECTED SEASONING

Georgia Frances King

58

SOFT LABOR: AN ILLUSTRATED GUIDE
TO SUMMER DREAM JOBS

Gail O'Hara

60

LINES IN THE SAND: A VIEW INTO THE WORLD
OF SAND ARTIST ANDRES AMADOR

Nirav Patel

68

RECIPE: BROWN BUTTER SALTED HONEY PIE

Kelsey Vala

70

SULTAN OF SALT: AN INTERVIEW
WITH MARK BITTERMAN

Kelsey Vala

74

BREAKING THE ICE: A SNOW CONE PRIMER

Lindsay Laricks

80

WHAT I LEARNED FROM THE SEA:
AN INTERVIEW WITH MARK KURLANSKY

Kelsey Vala

82

NAUTICAL INK: AN ILLUSTRATED GUIDE
TO MARITIME TATTOOS

Nikaela Marie Peters

84

THE SALT FLATS OF BOLIVIA: A PHOTO ESSAY
ON THE SALAR DE UYUNI SALT FLATS

Scarlett Hooft Graafland

FEW

92

THE SQUID FISHER'S HANDBOOK: A SERIES OF TIPS
ON HOW TO CATCH AND EAT A SQUID

James Bowden

94

LIFE ON THE WATER: WE VISIT THE HOMES OF
FOUR FAMILIES WHO LIVE BY THE SEA IN
ITALY, DENMARK, NEW ZEALAND AND MAINE

Georgia Frances King

———

112

A GUIDE TO FLIPPING: A PHOTO ESSAY THAT SHOWS
OFF THE SKILLS OF PROFESSIONAL DIVERS ALONG
WITH SOME UNPROFESSIONAL TIPS

Mark Sanders

118

THE CHANGING STATE OF THE SEA:
AN EDUCATIONAL ROUNDTABLE FROM A
PANEL OF UNDERWATER EXPERTS

122

THE CASE FOR CRYING: AN ESSAY ON
THE MEANING OF TEARS

Romy Ash

124

PERU'S SALTED PONDS: A TRAVEL PHOTO ESSAY
EXPLORING THE SALT POOLS NEAR MARAS

James Chororos

130

RECIPE: RICKY'S ENSENADA-STYLE FISH TACOS

Ricky Piña

132

KING OF THE CASTLE: AN INTERVIEW WITH ONE OF
THE WORLD'S FINEST SANDCASTLE BUILDERS

Georgia Frances King

134

A WHITER SHADE OF PALE: AN ESSAY ON
ENJOYING (AND ENDURING) THE SUNSHINE

Gail O'Hara

136

HIGH-RISE HARVEST: AN INTERVIEW WITH
ROOFTOP SALT MAKER SARAH SPROULE

Kelsey Vala

138

A CULINARY SALT ROUNDTABLE:
A SERIES OF QUOTES FROM CHEFS AND
FOOD WRITERS ON THE SEASONING

142

SALT AND VINEGAR MENU: SHAVED SUMMER
SQUASH SALAD WITH CHARRED CORN

Diana Yen

143

CREDITS

144

KEEP IN TOUCH

Ouur

We have some exciting news.

With the help of our readers, *Kinfolk* has been able to reach
some major milestones in just a few years. From cookbooks to gatherings,
we have grown a lot, and none of this would have been possible without you.

Now we'd like to offer you even more under a new collective brand that will
encompass publishing, apparel, community events, home goods and so much more.

Welcome to Ouur.

On Ouur's horizon:
An apparel and home goods collection, arriving soon.
Kinfolk Issue Thirteen, releasing in early September.
A second magazine, launching in late 2014.

Find out more:
OuurStudio.com

ONE

ENTERTAINING FOR ONE

o

THE SALINE SOLUTION

WORDS BY DANIEL CROCKETT & PHOTOGRAPH BY TEC PETAJA

We have more in common with seawater than we might imagine, so it's no wonder some of us feel more at home in the water than we do on land.

W e almost have salt water for blood. Humans share near-identical chemical levels of sodium chloride with the ocean, so it's no surprise that fishermen, sailors, surfers and wave watchers experience a connection that seems to go beyond the physical. For those to whom it whispers, the ocean can become a passion, a livelihood and a companion. Over time it starts to resemble a sort of second home. But it's a threatening place, unmapped at its depths, prone to hostile shifts in mood that trap the unwary, just like people do. Getting to know the sea is a lifelong challenge that's never truly complete, but it's also a journey back to where life began. By immersing ourselves in salt water, we bathe in our very origins. Maybe that's why surfing feels so… right.

Perhaps I'm maladjusted, but in the moving water the world makes sense. Our modern society of hyper-connectivity recedes from the frame. The sea strips us down to our basic elements and delivers us to the shore as different people, our chemical composure seemingly reset. Here we learn by osmosis that there's a plane beyond the visual, where the cultural stories we are blanketed with seem all the less relevant. We feel the rhythm of each set of waves: textures of a massive, flowing power.

"All of us have in our veins the exact same percentage of salt in our blood that exists in the ocean, and therefore we have salt in our blood, in our sweat, in our tears. We are tied to the ocean. And when we go back to the sea—whether it is to sail or to watch it—we are going back from whence we came" — JOHN F. KENNEDY

This quote isn't quite factually correct (our blood is 1 percent salinity while the sea has an average of 3.5 percent), but JFK's idea hit the mark: Longtime exposure to salt water creates a particular kind of connection with the floating world.

In the outer Orkney Islands off Northern Scotland, I once surfed a wave of extraordinary power delivered from Atlantic storms far away. With a bit of luck I raced along inside the wave, looking out at the cliffs and seals and pinwheeling birds. Encased in salt water, conscious thought stops. Time expands and distorts. The sound is an all-encompassing roar. I crouch and duck and contort, driving for the tightening exit, all without thinking. Each ocean lover has their own personal connection.

Many of us find an outlet in nature: a place where we feel truly at home, where there's no separation between us and the world. The ocean, chemically twinned with our blood, inspires a powerful bond that may even come to influence and reshape our conventional life. The might and majesty of the sea leaves us with the certain knowledge that we are part of something much greater. Yet for all the life-affirming, precious beauty of the saline landscape, it's a treacherous, challenging and sometimes downright adverse environment. But for those in touch with their saltwater blood, that's a great part of the allure. ○

Daniel Crockett is a surfer and writer who contributes to magazines such as Huck *and* The Surfer's Journal *and publishes* The Kook, *a fully analog newspaper. He currently lives in rural France.*

ROLLING IN THE DEEP

WORDS BY NIKAELA MARIE PETERS & PHOTOGRAPH BY BOBBY MILLS

There's poetry in the whale songs of the deep blue sea. You can hear their tune when you plant an ear below the water's surface, and if you concentrate, you can also listen to more of the ocean's secret rumblings.

It's August and a bowhead whale travels the legendary Northwest Passage. Until recently, this would've been impossible. But due to changes in climate and melting sea ice, she can now journey in summer across the high Canadian Arctic. From Pacific to Atlantic. From sea to shining sea.

Her ballad is lonely and remote. Like all whale songs, it has an otherworldly quality. If you were to anthropomorphize this beast, she'd be a woeful old soul, a victim of unrequited love, nostalgic and brave and wailing in the deep. She makes sound by moving air around inside her giant head. I wonder if this is therapeutic, like humming, if it drowns out pestering thoughts and sets a steady private rhythm. The sound waves carrying her song are silenced in the waves of the sea. If not recorded by divers or microphones strung under boats, her melody would remain locked under the ocean's surface.

Above the whale and unaware of her hymn, a sailboat passes. Until recently it was also unable to safely traverse this passage because of sea ice. The history of the Northwest Passage is a deadly one: For country and commerce, explorers have tried, failed and sometimes died trying to trace a shipping route above North America from Europe to Asia. Entire ships and their crews disappeared, most famously Sir John Franklin and his crew: Legend has it they were swallowed by ice in 1845. The Arctic is still the least explored ocean on earth. Even today, much remains obscure. To sail it is to live out every nine-year-old's dream of voyaging and discovering. Here you can be first.

Like the whale, the boat has a song: creaking rigging, droning engine, human voices. Personify this boat and she's all nerves, with a child's ambling imagination, naive and hopeful and skittish. She faces bleak odds and musters extreme courage. She's taking advantage of a small window of time: that magic moment each summer when the passage is sufficiently free of ice to sail. It's a temporary jubilee. Rules that ordinarily apply suddenly don't.

It's easy to understand the sailors' motives. They crave the unknown. They pursue the edges of human experience. They want adventure and glory. The whale's are more mysterious. What glory does she pursue? Does she contend with nature like us? Scientists have noticed that clans of bowheads from opposite oceans who used to be separated are now mingling. Greenlandic bowheads and Alaskan bowheads are meeting halfway. I wonder if each ocean's whales seek some plankton El Dorado, only to find each other instead? I imagine it as an emotional encounter: recognizing the call of another you've never met and hearing the history you share in their song.

So the moaning echoes and creaking rigging are added to the former quiet. The mournful sound of bagpipes in the deep, firsts and farewells and shifting frontiers. And so we beat on, boats and whales in the current, borne ceaselessly into a future we can't control or predict. ○

Nikaela Marie Peters is working on her master's degree in theology and has also studied philosophy, art and design. She lives in Winnipeg, Canada, with her husband and son.

ONE LAZY SUMMER

Summer is a time to lounge around and do as little as you can:
Sit in some trees, lie in the grass and stare at the clouds.
Here are a few more ways to watch the long days turn into night.

WORDS BY JULIE POINTER & PHOTOGRAPHS BY AGNES THOR

EXPAND YOUR HORIZONS
Submit to the wayward whims of the animal kingdom. Give friends a lift. Even the smallest things in nature are worth noticing.

SEEK DEPTH, NOT BREADTH

Choose your place and plant roots. Pick a patch of trees and learn them by heart. Watch the wind. Listen to summer's buzz.

GIVE THINGS TIME

Anything worth having rarely comes quickly. Choose patience and let the world around you unfold naturally. The joy of delayed gratification outweighs the waiting.

ENGAGE IN FAIR PLAY
The best amusements take some teamwork,
but there's always give and take. A little healthy
competition eggs us on, but forget winning:
Vie for most congenial this season.

MASTER A NEW HOBBY
Learn the language of rushing water. Pursue
something for the sake of the journey,
regardless of the final reward you may
(or may not) receive. ○

WRITING THE WAVES

WORDS BY NICOLE VILLENEUVE & PHOTOGRAPH BY ANJA VERDUGO

John Steinbeck may have once written that men need monsters in their personal oceans, but he also found a muse, a means of survival and a food source in the sea.

John Steinbeck's writing was nurtured by the waves. Whether he was wandering the streets of his hometown in Salinas, a 15-minute drive inland from the rocky beaches of northern California, or exploring the canneries of nearby Monterey, Steinbeck immersed himself in the culture of the coast. There he soaked up the details that would spill out into some of his greatest novels, such as *Tortilla Flat*, *East of Eden* and *Cannery Row*.

But to a writer just starting out, the Pacific also offered something more than inspiration: money. Steinbeck took odd jobs at fish hatcheries and on ocean freighters in order to fund his writing habit. Determined to break into East Coast publishing but short on cash, he took the sea-bound route to New York by working on a boat sailing through the Panama Canal. But he navigated back to the West Coast only a year later on the same waters: Rather than falling in love with the city, he fell for boats instead. "Thinking about a boat made the hair rise on the back of my neck," he once wrote to his editor, anxiously anticipating the day he'd be able to charter a craft of his own.

That time came after the publication of his 1935 breakout novel, *Tortilla Flat*. To celebrate, Steinbeck proudly purchased a small sailboat, the first vessel of his own. It crashed only a few years later, a victim of rough weather, but left the writer with an early taste of both the financial and physical freedom that he'd chase for the rest of his life. "I know what I want if my domestic difficulties and finances will permit it," he wrote in 1941, staring down his 40th birthday. "I want ten acres near the ocean… Then maybe I want a small boat. I suppose there isn't a chance in the world of having these."

These might sound like the average insecurities of a thirty-something writer looking toward an uncertain future, but by this stage Steinbeck, at 39, was arguably the most successful author in the country. Not only was *The Grapes of Wrath* the best-selling book of 1939, but it also won a Pulitzer and the National Book Award. Yet he wasn't content with the glory (or the royalties). Instead, he measured his happiness on the water.

In 1950, Steinbeck traded his beloved Pacific for the rocky shoreline of Long Island, whose whaling-town roots were still visible. This time, he was won over by the East Coast. He praised the variety of Atlantic seafood, relishing dinners of shad and bluefish he caught himself. "We bring them home alive and cook them while they are still kicking and they are delicious," he said. "My fear of starvation always disappears when I am near the ocean."

During these Sag Harbor years, water became not just a means of survival—or even a muse—but an essential part of the writing process itself. The ocean offered the solitude a writer needed to create and to dream. Instead of a room of his own, Steinbeck had a ship. "I can move out and anchor and have a little table and a yellow pad and some pencils," he said. "I can put myself in a position where nothing can intervene." From the choppy waters of the Long Island Sound, fishing line lazily trailing behind, he charted the course of his career, keeping his craft skimming along. ○

Nicole Villeneuve writes about food and literature from a tiny kitchen in New York City. She investigates the favorite recipes of famous authors at her website, Paper & Salt.

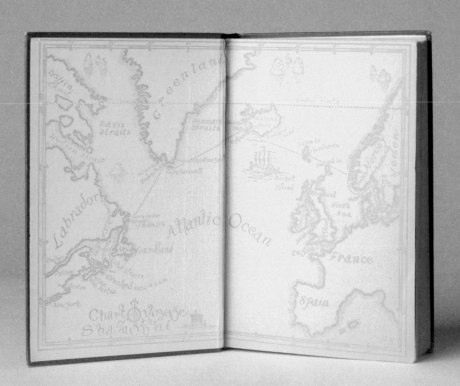

HOW TO BE NEIGHBORLY: TOWEL TERRITORY

A day at the beach should be filled with lazing and relaxation. However, as you're not the only one soaking up the sun, there are a few things to bear in mind to keep tempers cool.

WORDS BY GEORGIA FRANCES KING & ILLUSTRATIONS BY KATRIN COETZER

CLAIM YOUR SPACE (WITHIN REASON) Beach towels are the creators of sovereign seaside borders. The larger the surface area of your encampment, the larger empire you have in your terry-towel territory, free to govern as you so please. However, don't be a vacation Viking and invade other tanners' domains. Regardless of who set foot on your land first, be kind and keep the commandeering and pillaging to a minimum.

BRING ENOUGH FOOD TO SHARE Floating can be hungry work, and most people don't bring enough tasty food or fresh water to the beach. If your neighbor is picking at a sandy sandwich and you have some watermelon triangles to spare, do the right thing and offer the olive branch of communal dining: snacks. Besides, they may have the perfect bottle of Pimm's to match your glut of wilting fresh mint. Just don't do any of the above when there are seagulls circling, otherwise you'll risk a scrum of wings invading your Tupperware.

WALK THE WALK Sand is made up of billions of tiny worn-down particles of coral, rocks, shells, minerals and forgotten flip-flops. En masse they come together to provide us with a natural mattress on which to lie on and sun ourselves, but as individual elements they're prone to causing strife. Be careful not to kick up sand into your neighbors' eyes when wandering along the water's edge, shake out your towel at the end of the day in a secluded area and don't instigate sand-ball fights with toddlers.

SAY HELLO Cramming hundreds of people into a small space means the best way to survive a day sans awkwardness is acknowledging the absurdity of the human condition. After all, you're sharing a space with total strangers while wearing less clothing than you'd normally wear in front of your boss. Make sure you're not invading your neighbors' sandy solitude, but also don't ignore the semi-clad elephant in the room. A causal nod or a comment on the trashy novel they're reading will go far for niceties, and then you can return to your mutual ignoring.

PLAY BALL WITHIN BOUNDS Being at the beach can be an easy way to get some incidental exercise. In between rounds of rotisserie tanning, ask to join in on a volleyball game or start throwing a Frisbee around (just alert your nearby sunbathers first so you don't wind up with several rhinoplasty bills). However, if you were blessed with two left feet or the hand-eye coordination of a preschooler, leave the ball sports to those who can aim away from the slumbering elders. ○

Georgia Frances King has recently swapped her sweltering Australian summers for the cool river breezes of Portland, Oregon. She is the editor of Kinfolk *and a seasoned beach napper.*

THE ONE THAT GOT AWAY

WORDS BY DAVID COGGINS & PHOTOGRAPH BY THE WEAVER HOUSE

For some, going fishing is about bringing home the salmon. For others, it's simply about the possibility of a catch. Life is about casting a wide net, and sometimes the important part isn't what ends up in it.

Fishing is a curious pursuit. You set yourself up for failure again and again, though the embarrassment comes in different forms and still manages to surprise you. Of course there's always a remote chance of success, but take a photo when that happens or nobody will believe you. All of which is to say that anglers remain improbable optimists at heart.

We hope against hope that this time it will be different. We try our luck against the odds, but we also have to deal with the metaphors: There's the one that got away, of course. But don't worry, there's always another fish in the sea. Or maybe it goes back to obsession and *Moby Dick*. But the metaphors are often too much: Sometimes a fish is just a fish.

My first saltwater quarry was not fish at all, but crab. As young kids we visited my grandparents' house on a canal in south Texas. My sister and I would run downstairs first thing each morning to haul out the crab trap that hung off the dock. It was a big chicken-wire cube with openings at each end and a cylinder in the center full of some gnarly chicken meat my grandmom stuck in it.

The crabs entered through the openings, fell down to the bottom and couldn't climb out. We never understood the physics of the thing (or why crabs like chicken), but we loved to see their blue shells when we pulled the trap out of the water, even though we were frightened of their claws and the strange way their color shifted in the sun like gasoline. When crabs were served at dinner, my sister and I abstained: We didn't even like crabs—we held out for fried shrimp. But the catch was the thing. The anticipation gives you a high, kind of like scratching off a lottery ticket.

That may not qualify as fishing; the trap does all the work and you just show up to check on it. But I was already obsessed with the possibility of success. When I got older, I'd hang a lure over the edge of the dock, and then catch an ugly gray catfish if I was lucky. They have sharp barbels that look like whiskers, and I'd stare at these prehistoric faces before I made my Uncle Bill unhook them and throw them back in the water.

Just fishing was enough. But as you learn more you expect more, and you rarely get the results you feel you deserve. The remarkable thing about fishing is its incredible capacity, despite your experience, to make you feel like a novice. The more you know, the more you realize you have to learn. Wait, is that another metaphor?

When you're young, you're happy for any action and every fish looks big. These days I don't troll for catfish in Texas—I fly-fish for trout in Montana—but the impulse is the same. You like the mystery of what's happening beneath the surface and the first sight of the fish when it comes out of the water. It's enough to make you comfortable with failure, because you know your luck can change with the next cast. ○

David Coggins is a writer who lives in New York. His work has appeared in Esquire, Interview *and the* Wall Street Journal, *among other places. When he does get lucky on the river, he throws the fish back.*

SWIMMING WITH SHARKS

WORDS BY KATE MAYES & PHOTOGRAPHS BY TEC PETAJA

In certain coastal areas of the world, shark sightings are a commonplace occurrence that you trade for a day at the sea. But it's important to remember that it's their home we're swimming in, not ours.

I like to think of Western Australia as the Wild West: Its people are braver by nature and have tighter connections to the land and its creatures. After all, we swim with sharks.

Not really. Not all the time, at least, and not usually by choice. But that's what I tell my East Coast friends as I look out at the surging waves of Bronte Beach. It may just be sentimental patriotism for my home state, but I like to stir the pot of the Sydney city slickers.

It's been more than a year since I swam in the Australian ocean. I blame work. I blame my chaotic schedule. I even blame travel. These excuses are weak. It's like I've forgotten how important the sea once was to me. Truth be told, I'm more afraid of facing the waves than the possibility of finding sharks in these particular waters. Their peaks roar into shore one after the other with no particular rhyme or rhythm, a chaos of white froth, salt and sand. Like Homer's sirens, they egg me on but also give me a subtle warning.

They have started culling the sharks in Australia: We love the ocean that much. There have been seven fatal attacks in three years in Western Australia alone. They say we've got to kill the sharks to stop our deaths. They say we need to feel confident to go back into the water.

But those salty shallows are their habitat, not ours. And I say that it's our risk to swim in them, not theirs. The irony of it plays over in my mind as I look out across the ocean. Sharks breathe that water in. They quite literally have to swim to breathe. But we want a piece of it too. Australians cling to shorelines as though life depended on it.

It's the risk I choose to take as I stand at the water's edge. I twirl to look back up the beach to where my friends are sitting, reapplying their lotions and pulling out their books. I wade in. It takes a powerful push to make it through the first breaks. I search for the wave to dive into and take me to the other side without kissing the ocean floor in a swirl of sand.

There's a silence that comes in that moment when you pierce the surface. Your chest stretches out like the wings of a seabird. Your body takes control of your underwater existence, as though nature had designed it that way. For those few moments, I feel like a creature of the sea.

And then I remember that I'm not: salt water in my nose, eyes and mouth. It's nature's gentle reminder that I'm just a visitor in these waters and that, unlike the sharks, I don't belong here.

Eventually I take the message and head back through the shallows to the sandy shore. I usually bathe in the freshwater showers, but not today. I want to drive home with the salt on my skin and in my hair. I want to see it on the bathroom floor later that night, to remind me the next day and the day after that the sea is there.

It's always there. But only for me to borrow. And that sometimes, like a shark, I have to swim to breathe. ○

Kate Mayes works in the Australian publishing industry and also writes for children under the pen name Ruthie May. She lives in the inner city of Sydney, but her first love will always be the Western Australia coastline.

THE SALT AND VINEGAR MENU

---

*Anyone who has ever had salt and vinegar chips can attest
that this combination is delicious, especially when served with
a cold beer or iced tea. We built a menu around the classic
pairing and came up with these simple dishes.*

SHAVED SUMMER SQUASH
SALAD WITH CHARRED CORN

STUFFED SALT AND
VINEGAR POTATO SKINS

GRILLED CHICKEN WITH
BLACKBERRY BALSAMIC SAUCE

RECIPES & FOOD STYLING BY DIANA YEN & THE JEWELS OF NEW YORK
PHOTOGRAPHS BY ALICE GAO & PROP STYLING BY KATE S. JORDAN

Recipe for Shaved Summer Squash Salad with Charred Corn on page 142

THE SALT AND VINEGAR MENU

STUFFED SALT AND VINEGAR POTATO SKINS

The idea for this recipe came from a desire to update the old-school snack food found in most strip-mall chain restaurants and give it a fresh twist. Even in summer, we always want to come up with new ways to eat crispy potatoes covered in delicious cheesy and creamy toppings.

*6 small to medium-size russet potatoes
(about 3 pounds / 1.4 kilograms)*

*1/2 cup (120 milliliters) white wine vinegar,
plus more for serving*

Extra-virgin olive oil, for brushing

8 ounces (225 grams) sharp white cheddar, shredded

Freshly ground black pepper, to taste

8 ounces (225 grams) crème fraîche

Chopped parsley, to garnish

Smoked sea salt, to taste

METHOD Scrub the potatoes clean and cut in half lengthwise. Place the potatoes in a large stockpot and cover with cold water. Bring the potatoes just to a simmer and continue simmering for about 25 minutes until tender but still firm. Set aside to cool. Scoop out the flesh into a bowl, leaving a 1/4-inch thick shell. The potato flesh may be set aside for another use. Lightly score the interior of each potato and brush generously with vinegar, allowing the flavors to soak in.

Preheat the grill to medium heat.

Brush the potato skins with olive oil and season with salt and pepper. Place on the grill, skin side up and cook for 2–3 minutes, until golden. Turn the potatoes over and grill for 5 minutes longer. During the last few minutes of grilling, sprinkle each potato with the cheese and cook until melted.

Garnish with the crème fraîche and parsley, and finish with smoked sea salt. Serve with more vinegar as desired. ○

Serves 6

THE SALT AND VINEGAR MENU

GRILLED CHICKEN WITH BLACKBERRY BALSAMIC SAUCE

G rilled chicken is a summertime staple at every backyard barbecue. The key to great chicken is to marinate it before grilling to add a depth of flavor and to seal in the moisture while cooking. We've added a twist to this classic dish with our sweet and tangy blackberry balsamic sauce.

FOR THE CHICKEN	FOR THE BLACKBERRY BALSAMIC SAUCE
1/2 cup (120 milliliters) extra-virgin olive oil	*2 teaspoons (10 grams) extra-virgin olive oil*
Zest and juice of 2 lemons	*1 garlic clove, minced*
2 tablespoons (30 grams) Dijon mustard	*1/4 cup (25 grams) finely minced shallot*
2 tablespoons (40 grams) honey	*2 cups (225 grams) blackberries*
3 garlic cloves, peeled	*1 cup (235 milliliters) balsamic vinegar*
1 tablespoon (3 grams) fresh thyme leaves	*1/2 cup (170 grams) honey*
Salt and black pepper, to taste	*Salt and pepper, to taste*
2 whole chickens (about 3 pounds / 1.4 kilograms each), cut into 8 pieces each	

METHOD In a bowl, combine the olive oil, lemon zest and juice, mustard, honey, garlic, thyme, salt and pepper. Transfer into a resealable plastic bag. Place the chicken inside the bag and coat evenly with the marinade. Seal tightly and store in the refrigerator for an hour.

Meanwhile, heat the olive oil in a small saucepan and stir in the garlic and shallots until tender, about 2 minutes. Add the blackberries, balsamic vinegar and honey. Bring to a boil over medium-high heat, then lower and simmer uncovered for 5–10 minutes until sauce thickens. Add salt and pepper to taste.

Preheat the grill to medium heat and lightly oil the grate.

Remove the chicken from the marinade, discarding the bag and its remaining contents. Pat the chicken dry. Cook the chicken on the preheated grill until cooked through with an internal temperature of 165°F (74°C), approximately 7–8 minutes on each side.

Arrange the grilled chicken on a platter and drizzle with the blackberry balsamic sauce. ○

Serves 6

BRITISH BEACH TOWNS: A SOCIAL HISTORY

WORDS BY TRAVIS ELBOROUGH & PHOTOGRAPH BY JOSEPH CONWAY

Beach resort towns in the United Kingdom no longer have "wheeled bathing machines" and seawater as medicine, but there are a number of characteristics they still do share.

Great Britain possesses some 11,072 miles of coastline. Wherever you stand in the United Kingdom, you are rarely more than 72 miles from a beach. So it's no surprise that the seaside holiday, like soccer and the railways, was a British invention. And as with soccer and the railways, the rest of the world (mostly blessed with more space and better weather) went off and improved on it. Here's a tour of the features that still characterize a classic British seaside town.

THE BEACH Who doesn't feel better on a beach? The dusty feel of sand and an expanse of undulating greeny-blue sea? Doesn't it all sound so inviting, invigorating even? Some 200 years ago, doctors in coastal towns such as Brighton certainly thought so: Back then they began prescribing bathing in and drinking seawater as a cure for ailments such as gout. The beach resort was born! Thankfully we don't drink seawater today (and what the hell is gout?) but the seaside remains a place we all go to recuperate.

THE PIER The earliest seaside piers were simple timber jetties for passenger boats, but in most resorts in Britain they evolved into magnificent promenades. Jutting out into the sea like inky exclamation points, the grandest at Great Yarmouth, Eastbourne, Blackpool and Brighton are as fantastical as anything in *Alice in Wonderland*. Their wide-decked walkways boast quasi-Oriental domed booths, theaters and bars. With the waves swirling beneath, you can imagine being on an ocean liner only a few hundred yards from land. And how often is anyone given the chance to walk on water?

BEACH HUTS In the 19th century, when seemingly a bare table leg was deemed shocking, female beachgoers were urged to "preserve their modesty" by entering the water inside timber shacks on wheels called "bathing machines." As more liberated women abandoned these machines for knitted bathing costumes, the huts were refashioned as seafront chalets. Brightly painted rows of these enchantingly Lilliputian houses now appear on British beachfronts like displays of frosted cakes.

FISH AND CHIPS This is a meal that tastes best by the beach. Ideally it should be eaten straight out of the paper it's wrapped in, using a wooden fork to prong morsels of white fillet and fried potato into the mouth so that the pungent aromas of vinegar and caramelized batter mingle with the damp, briny sea air. Like many great British dishes, it owes its origins to immigrants: The battered fish was introduced by Spanish and Portuguese Jews, while fried chipped potatoes were a staple among migrant Irish laborers.

PUNCH AND JUDY PUPPET SHOWS Mr. Punch is a puppet with a carved wooden head shaped like a crescent moon whose shows have been performed in Britain for more than 300 years. He can be spied on beaches every summer beating his wife Judy, their baby and a crocodile with a chunk of lumber before a puppet cop finally intervenes. Go figure.

THE RAIN British beachfronts all glimmer with the light from amusement arcades reminiscent of old traveling fairgrounds. These gaudy halls full of slot machines, all blinking and beeping away lasciviously, are perfect for an hour or two when it rains. And it always rains. ○

Descended from a family of coastal dwellers who pioneered pirate-themed eateries and shell-shaded electric lamps, Travis Elborough has written books including Wish You Were Here: England on Sea.

TAFFY TALES

WORDS BY CARLY DIAZ & PHOTOGRAPH BY ANJA VERDUGO

The term "salt water taffy" may be somewhat misleading, but the name stuck to the candy like it sticks to your teeth. Sure, some variations may contain a bit of salt, but salt water has never been used in the chewy treats. We explored the history of taffy to find out how it got its name.

According to legend, salt water taffy originated in 1883 on the boardwalk in Atlantic City, New Jersey, when candy shop proprietor David Bradley discovered his confectionery inventory had been soaked by the Atlantic waves during a huge storm. Searching for a way to save his livelihood, he urged the first customer of the day to try his new invention: salt water taffy. Was it David's sister who overheard him and sensed a marketing opportunity in the name? Or maybe the taffy-loving customer flaunted the limited-edition treat to her friends up and down the boardwalk?

However the circumstances unfolded, the transformation from everyday taffy to the beloved "salt water" variety quickly took root. But it was fellow Atlantic City confectioner and entrepreneur Joseph Fralinger who is credited with taking the newly minted candy and making it a household name a few years later. He began selling boxes of salt water taffy to tourists as boardwalk souvenirs and its fame quickly spread. Competitors quickly followed—kicking off the resort town's infamous copyright-driven "taffy wars"—which spurred innovation in production and the expansion of flavors from traditional molasses, chocolate and vanilla to root beer, sour cherry, creamsicle and dozens more.

Early confectioners endured the labor-intensive process of pulling, stretching, cutting and wrapping individual candies by hand. Their hard work resulted in taffy that was infused with air, giving it a light texture and trademark chewiness. In 1912, the process was streamlined with the invention of the pulling machine, which twisted and aerated the taffy to an even softer consistency. As mass production increased, the association of salt water taffy with a trip to the ocean was cemented. The appeal of the treat conjures up memories of the beach and a taste of the ocean that melts in your mouth, even if the presence of salt water is just pure legend.

The production of salt water taffy is still a source of pride for many beachfront confectioners. We've put together a list of places to get your fill of taffy. ○

SALT WATER TAFFY CO.
Half Moon Bay, California
A waterfront shop with more than 50 flavors of salt water taffy.

FRALINGER'S
Atlantic City, New Jersey
Home of the original Atlantic City souvenir.

SALTY ROAD
Brooklyn, New York
This modern taffy maker pulls soft, creamy taffy with a distinct salt crystal crunch in flavors such as salty caramel apple and bergamot.

BRUCE'S CANDY KITCHEN
Seaside, Oregon
Family-owned for more than 80 years, this place has a pulling machine that dates back to 1923.

MEHLENBACHER'S TAFFY
Paso Robles, California
Uses a recipe from 1900 and all taffy is pulled by hand as natural flavors are added.

WEE·R·SWEETZ
Myrtle Beach, South Carolina
Family-owned for more than 30 years and made while you watch.

ZENO'S
Daytona Beach, Florida
Family-owned since 1948, Zeno's uses a special whipping technique for even softer taffy.

AINSLEE'S
Depoe Bay, Oregon
A waterfront shop since 1937 with more than 31 flavors.

Or for similar sweets, try *caramelo masticable* in Spain, *Tire de la Sainte-Catherine* in France, *shinmoto* in Japan, *keo kéo* in Vietnam or *yeot* in Korea.

TWO

ENTERTAINING FOR TWO

○ ○

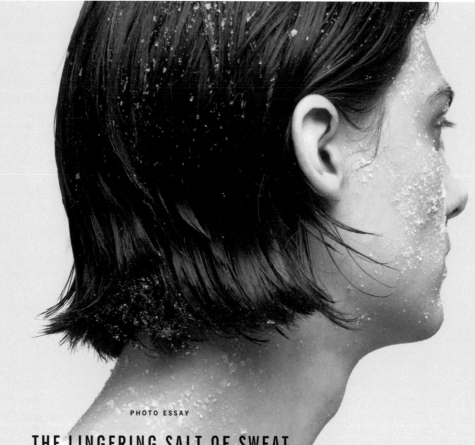

THE LINGERING SALT OF SWEAT

A trip to the seaside means immersing yourself in nature's salty bath and basking in the summer heat. As the ocean and salt crystals dry on your skin, they leave behind a memory of the day that was.

PHOTOGRAPHS BY CHARLIE SCHUCK & STYLING BY ASHLEY HELVEY

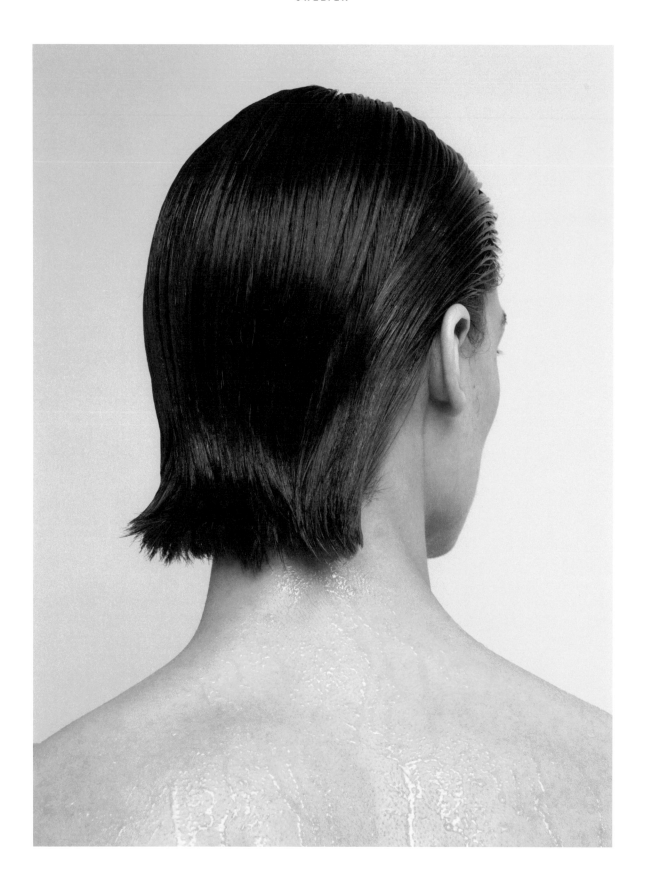

A LETTER FROM PEPPER

WORDS BY GEORGIA FRANCES KING & PHOTOGRAPH BY ANJA VERDUGO

Dear Salt,

I have a bone to pick with you. If we're going to continue sharing the same space on the table, as we have been civilly for centuries, it's only fair that we start addressing the recent development of your superiority complex. I've been undermined as the lesser shaker for far too long, so I think it's time to balance the seasonings.

You've become such a cosmopolitan harlot. Everyone can't stop harping on about French fleur de sel this, Himalayan rock salt that. But while you go around whoring yourself out to any salty body of water available, I was once a commodity that could only be sourced from faraway Asia.

In fact, part of the reason the Americas were even stumbled upon again by European explorers is that my exotic presence was in such high demand. Europe was so hooked on Indian spices throughout the Middle Ages that they were all competing to find the best trade route to my homeland. While most were sailing east, Christopher Columbus reckoned the world was round and thereby figured he could sail west and eventually hit Asia. And he would've if the Bahamas hadn't been in his way. So you have *me* to thank that there's even an American rack for you to be dominating.

And don't go saying, "Oh! But Pepper! The body needs salt! I'm saving lives!" Sure, but not *that* much. You silent sham, you sly seasoning, sitting on all those beer nuts, unknowingly dehydrating those innocent men and women, forcing them into a liquor-laden stupor… Most humans are eating far too much of you, and more than two-thirds comes from you sneaking yourself into nearly all processed foods from sliced bread to canned tomatoes. You raise blood pressure. You heighten the risk of hypertension. You can give people kidney disease. The worst I ever did was make someone sneeze.

You've instigated far more trouble than me: You've caused wars. France's salt tax helped start the French Revolution. You upped the ante in America's Revolutionary War when the British intercepted vital salt shipments. When Gandhi led India's law-defying Salt Satyagraha in 1930, it took the nation's revolt into the hands of the people. Yes, you may have stoked the fire of revolutions, but you've hurt people in the process. There's a reason behind that old saying about salt and wounds.

Did you know I was once more valuable than gold? That's right, don't look so shocked. I was the measure of wealth for nearly a millennium in Europe: You could pay rent, taxes, dowries or bribes in peppercorns. A pound of pepper would free a slave in France, ancient Greeks used me as currency and it was said I cured impotency in the first century. In the fifth century, Alaric (King of the Visigoths) weaseled Italy out of a bounty that included 3,000 pounds of pepper—no salt to be mentioned. Even Sir Paul McCartney prefers me: Whoever heard of Sgt. Salt's Lonely Hearts Club Band?

And finally, as if you needed any more proof of my eminence, I'm the one who's encased in the holy scepter of fine dining: the freshly cracked pepper mill. My aroma has been deemed so powerful by the culinary gods that only a waiter may wield me. And where are you? Sitting in that lonely little bowl on the table with a dozen dirty fingers pinching at you like a flock of pigeons.

So think about it, Salt. You need to take your ego with a grain of yourself.

Yours Sincerely,

Pepper

SOFT LABOR

The best summer jobs involve getting paid while you still have the wind of freedom blowing through your hair.

WORDS BY GAIL O'HARA &
ILLUSTRATIONS BY SARAH BURWASH

Fun summer job might be an oxymoron for most, but in these recessionary times, we all have to be wide open to doing all kinds of work. Why should face painting, taffy pulling and pool watching be jobs reserved for teenagers? Should work be fun? We say *yes indeed*.

JOIN THE CIRCUS If you want to stay childlike, working at a carnival, boardwalk or amusement park is the way to go. Starving artists can spend their days drawing caricatures or painting funny faces on children, and those who like to play with their food would be lucky to land a gig working at a chocolate factory or making cotton candy all day.

GET OUT For some, getting out into nature, to the country or near the water provides the best office space. Being a camp counselor may not be the top-grossing position of all time, but spending all your time creating s'more recipes and racing canoes will more than make up for it. You could also be a lifeguard: They're usually golden brown and in tip-top shape (which often helps with other aspects of your social life). Organic farming or working at a plant nursery can be excellent learning experiences too, and the same goes for being a surfboard renter or a park ranger.

LISTEN UP For music fans, spending the summer working in a record store can be a smart way to keep up on all the best albums coming out. It also ensures that you'll be around plenty of fellow music nerds to argue with about the latest St. Vincent LP. But there's always a danger of spending your entire paycheck on rare vinyl before you even get paid! Another fun gig for music-intensive types would be to sell merchandise for your favorite band while they're on tour, though sometimes getting to know them may kill your deep admiration. Just email them: If they don't need a merch seller, perhaps you can become a soundperson's protégé.

CITY SLICKERS If you're stuck in a big city, there are loads of entertaining jobs even if you don't snag a fancy internship. Top options include working at a food cart, driving a popsicle truck, running a paddleboat rental business or becoming a dog walker. What better way to spend your summer than being pulled around town by a pack of adorable mutts?

INSIDE TRACK When it comes to summer, most of us would rather be outside doing anything other than sitting in an office. But some folks prefer the darkness, air-conditioning and escaping the icky humidity, so there's nothing more wonderful than sitting inside your chilled living room testing video games all summer long. It might not be the greatest for your back, eyes or health, but for some people it's definitely a dream gig. Another dark place to stay cool and unsweaty is inside a local cinema: Try being a projectionist—or better yet an usher—so you can sneakily watch all the summer blockbusters while doing very little actual work. ○ ○

LINES IN THE SAND

*San Francisco native Andres Amador paints with sand. After scouting
remote beaches up and down the California coastline, he takes to them
with little more than an idea and a rake to create these meditative images.
We follow him as he turns the seashore into his canvas.*

PHOTOGRAPHS BY NIRAV PATEL

Based in San Francisco, Andres Amador creates installations, sells prints of his work and teaches workshops on playa (Spanish for beach) painting. Learn more at andresamadorarts.com

BROWN BUTTER SALTED HONEY PIE

RECIPE BY KELSEY VALA & PHOTOGRAPH BY HANNAH MENDENHALL
STYLING BY ANNE PARKER

We've recently been hooked on the salted honey pie from Sweedeedee in Portland, Oregon, and Four & Twenty Blackbirds in Brooklyn, so we created our own version with nutty browned butter and large flakes of sea salt to balance the honey's floral notes.

FOR THE CRUST

1/2 cup (115 grams) very cold unsalted butter, cut into 1/2-inch cubes

1/2 cup (120 milliliters) ice water

1 1/2 teaspoons (8 grams) white sugar

1 1/4 cups (160 grams) all-purpose flour, plus more for dusting

1/2 teaspoon (3 grams) salt

1 egg beaten with a splash of water for egg wash

FOR THE FILLING

3/4 cup (1 1/2 sticks / 170 grams) unsalted butter

3/4 cup (255 grams) honey (lavender or orange blossom are ideal)

1 cup (200 grams) granulated sugar

2 tablespoons (15 grams) all-purpose flour

3/4 teaspoon (4 grams) salt

1 tablespoon (15 milliliters) lemon juice

5 large eggs

2 teaspoons (10 grams) pure vanilla extract or vanilla paste

1 cup (235 milliliters) heavy cream

Flaky sea salt for topping

METHOD For the crust: In a large bowl, whisk together the flour, sugar and salt. Sprinkle the cubed butter into the flour mixture, and using your hands or pastry blender, begin working the butter into the flour. Once the butter is a little bigger than pea-size pebbles, start drizzling in half of the water and incorporating it into the flour mixture with your hands or a spatula. Drizzle in more water 1 tablespoon at a time until the dough comes together. Gently knead the dough on a lightly floured work surface and shape into a disk. Wrap the disk in plastic wrap and place in the refrigerator for at least 1 hour. When ready, roll the crust to 1/8-inch thickness and transfer to 10-inch pie pan and crimp. Cover with plastic wrap and let the piecrust chill in the refrigerator for at least 1 more hour. Just before filling, brush the entire crust with the egg wash.

For the filling: Preheat the oven to 350°F (177°C). Melt the butter in a saucepan over medium heat. The butter will start to simmer and foam. As the foam subsides, stir the butter constantly and watch for it to turn golden and then brown, about 10 minutes. Once it turns brown, quickly remove from heat, add the honey and stir until it dissolves. Let the mixture cool slightly, about 10 minutes.

Whisk together the sugar, flour and salt in a medium-size bowl. Stir in the brown butter, vanilla paste and lemon juice, and whisk until thoroughly combined. Add the eggs, one at a time, whisking after each addition. Whisk in the heavy cream.

Pour the filling into the chilled piecrust. Bake the pie on the center rack in the oven for 60 to 75 minutes, rotating the pie halfway through baking. The pie is done when it turns deep golden brown on top. It should be puffed up and set around the edges but should still slightly jiggle in the center. Let rest at room temperature for at least 4 hours. Sprinkle with flaky sea salt. ○ ○

SULTAN OF SALT

WORDS BY KELSEY VALA

PHOTOGRAPHS BY ANAÏS & DAX (PAGE 70) & ANJA VERDUGO (PAGE 73)

Salt has been around forever, but you still might say that Mark Bitterman put it on the map. We interview him about food writing, food eating and a lifelong love affair with the sea, chocolate, salt and bitters.

Mark Bitterman has pioneered a new way of thinking about salt, the ubiquitous mineral that once was just an afterthought on our dinner plates. With an obsession that began long ago in France, Mark is now a trained salt professional and academic (called a *selmelier)*. He has gone on to write a historical guidebook called *Salted: A Manifesto on the World's Most Essential Mineral, With Recipes*, and is co-owner of the Meadow, a specialty boutique that sells salts, chocolates and bitters from around the world with locations in Portland, Oregon, and New York City's West Village. We asked this salt scholar to share a pinch of his salty knowledge along with some personal stories.

WHAT DO YOU LIKE TO COOK AT HOME?

I cook pretty simply at home but usually with inspiration from more exotic experiences. I just got back from Turkey and South Africa, and one of the most incredible things I tasted was a cup of pomegranate juice I bought while looking for breakfast in the fish markets in Istanbul, squeezed on the spot by a street vendor with a rickety wooden cart. The juice was frosty, exhilarating and electrically intense. I can't get it out of my head. Lately it's been finding its way into everything I make: pork with mild chilies and pomegranate reduction, corn bread with pomegranate freezer jam, fennel salad and pomegranate seeds…

WHAT KINDS OF SIMPLE MEALS DO YOU EAT ON A NORMAL WEEKNIGHT?

Pomegranate! Actually, I almost never follow a recipe. I cook by feel, taking recipes only as inspiration or for an understanding of the foundation of the dish. In summer and fall I grill just about everything: ribs, artichokes, whole fish, oranges, peppers, romaine. The Frenchy in me loves sauces, so there's usually something drizzled on top—plus making sauces is a great way to make a dent in my absurdly huge collection of condiments. In the winter and spring I definitely go for comfort: something delicate like lamb or fish, or a beef roast with insane amounts of garlic and caramelized root vegetables, or a bone-in pork shoulder cooked all day at 190 degrees with a mess of spices, sugar, salt and vinegar. Winter cooking should boast as many calories as can gracefully be brought to bear.

WHAT WOULD YOU MAKE FOR FRIENDS COMING OVER?

I have guests over a few times a week, and usually I just involve them in whatever I'm cooking. For better or worse, my efforts are not on entertainment, but on feeding people and making them feel at home. The big difference is the cocktail: There's no more powerful way to make someone feel at home— or to get them hungry—than to put a carefully made cocktail in their hands.

WHO ARE SOME PEOPLE YOU'VE MET WHILE TRAVELING WHO INSPIRED YOU?

The most inspirational cook of my life was Angel, a beautiful old woman who fled the famines of Mussolini and eventually established herself as the nanny and housekeeper at a château in southwestern France where I lived for a number of years. She knew some exquisite country French dish for every occasion. Six dozen pigeons netted in an old barn = pigeon over coals with fig jam. The leftover head of a wild boar I shot = *daube de sanglier* drowned in two bottles of Fitou wine. Bushels of morels brought by the neighbor = a marriage with a goat-milk Brie from the Pyrenees. Inquiries into her techniques were met with, "Just a little salt and pepper."

DO YOU USE HIMALAYAN SALT BLOCKS TO COOK ON A DAILY BASIS?

Himalayan salt blocks (pictured) have settled onto most of the surfaces in my kitchen, and I use them pretty much daily. I keep the butter out by the stove on a four-inch-thick cube of salt that keeps it cool even when the stove gets hot. Appetizers like radishes and butter, fruit and cheese, and olives and meats are almost always served on a salt block, as are many salads, whether it's avocados and cucumbers or pears and endive. I cook on salt blocks whenever the food warrants it: Scallops, duck breast and shrimp in their shells simply don't compare in a pan. If I'm having guests over, I use salt blocks more deliberately because their primordial beauty contributes to the atmosphere of hospitality and chitchat.

WHEN WAS THE FIRST TIME YOU REALLY NOTICED SALT?

It was a steak I ate in France, served with French gray sea salt. It blew me away: big silvery, crunchy, briny crystals studding a thick, succulently juicy steak. I'd never before seen salt as a distinctive thing, a kinetic ingredient, an unfolding story. This experience was followed by a bunch of other discoveries at about the same time, like fleur de sel in hand-churned butter and caramels, an Italian sea salt called "sweet salt" that actually tastes like berries just because of the strange *meroir* of the Adriatic, and mines in Austria that still harbor 3,000-year-old mummified rock salt miners.

PLEASE DESCRIBE THE MOST MEMORABLE MEAL OF YOUR LIFE.

Lord, that's a doozy. I just ate at Atera in New York with my two friends. The food was beyond brilliant: 20 courses of smart, inventive, elegant bites. Trout liver followed by trout flesh followed by trout roe followed by a lobster roll that imploded on the tongue and lashed out flavor with the electromagnetic force of a quasar. But it's probably the simplest meals I really remember the best: sitting with my father and some friends at a picnic bench in Tuscany where they served lardo and lemon-cured anchovies; my first son pushing his plate of mushed veggies aside and eating the two adult portions of sole I had cooked up; or a roast with potatoes served to me by the wife of a man who picked me up on the side of the road in the Rockies after my motorcycle broke down.

WHY DID YOU BECOME A FOOD WRITER?

It had never occurred to me to write about food until I grew frustrated with the lack of information and critical thinking about salt. There was just so much undocumented information, unshared experience and passion that had to get out. Once I started writing about salt, it felt like the floodgates had been opened. Salt is the most ancient, universal, powerful and versatile ingredient in the world. Eventually I got over the intimidation of taking on such a subject and did my best to give it the attention it deserved.

YOU COINED THE TERM *SELMELIER*. HOW DOES THIS WORD DEFINE WHAT YOU DO?

My job is to guide people toward a tastier, more vital, more relevant connection to their food. I do this through salt because it's the only food eaten by every culture everywhere in the world. The word was inspired by the term *sommelier*, which is not just a wine expert but a server whose job is to enrich your experience of food. Of course, salt is more important than wine! Martinis are a superb fuel for motoring through a fine meal in the absence of wine—or beer will do in a pinch—but salt is indispensable, and often more surprising and illuminating.

AS JAMES BEARD ONCE ASKED, "WHERE WOULD WE BE WITHOUT SALT?"

A wise man! And a fellow Oregonian. Salt is nature's way of showing enthusiasm. Salting food celebrates the pleasure offered to us in life. ○ ○

BREAKING THE ICE: A SNOW CONE PRIMER

*You shouldn't have to stop enjoying the sugar high and psychedelic colors
of snow cones just because you've grown up. We enlisted the help
of professional snow cone maker Lindsay Laricks to come up
with some modern variations of those icy treats.*

WORDS & RECIPES BY LINDSAY LARICKS
PHOTOGRAPHS BY KATHRIN KOSCHITZKI

FROSTY TIPS

TOOLS

Maker: The easiest way to make snow cones is using small machines found at many home stores. A more authentic option is the *raspador de hielo* (a small handheld metal shaver used by many street vendors in Mexico). You can also try using a blender, but it'll dull the blade over time.

Vessels: Paper cones are available online and at office supply shops. If you want to use glasses, then short and squat ones (like a rocks glass) are best so you don't have to dig down to get to the bottom of the shaved ice. Personally, I use 9-ounce compostable plastic cups, which are easy to eat out of and kind to the environment.

Scoop: You'll need something to scoop and shape the shaved ice with (an ice cream scoop works great).

MAKING THE ICE

Using a machine: Follow the directions for each product.

Using a raspador de hielo: Make a big block of ice by freezing water in a plastic container. Run it along the top of the block to make some fluffy snow.

Using a blender: You can make coarse ice using a blender, but be aware that it can be rough on the machine.

TIPS

If all of your ingredients are kept cold before use, it will help your ice stay intact and not melt. If you're using alcohol it will instantly melt the ice, so for boozy snow cones put the alcohol at the bottom first, topping with shaved ice second and then finishing with the homemade syrup: This way you can have a boozy snow cone that still maintains a cute shape. When serving, let people know the alcohol is at the bottom so they can stir.

GARNISHES

These give everything a nice finishing touch, so enjoy brainstorming whatever might complement your flavors. A citrus twist? A drizzle of sweetened condensed milk? A sprig of fresh herbs? Color, flavor and aroma should be your guide.

MOJITO

2 cups (475 milliliters) lime juice*

1 cup (235 milliliters) water

3 cups (600 grams) pure cane sugar

A few sprigs of fresh mint

Powdered sugar for dusting

White rum (approx. 1 ounce / 30 milliliters per person)

- - -

METHOD Combine the lime juice, water and sugar at room temperature until the sugar is dissolved. Do not heat, as citrus can get pretty bitter if heated. Finely mince the mint and mix it into the syrup so that you have little bits of fresh mint in each bite. Immediately pour into a clean glass bottle or jar and refrigerate.

TO SERVE Pour 1 ounce (30 milliliters) of rum into the bottom of your cup. Fill with shaved ice. Sculpt the top into a nice round shape. Drizzle 2–3 ounces (60–90 milliliters) of the mojito mix over the top. Dust with powdered sugar and add a sprig of fresh mint.

*Key lime juice is ideal for this recipe, as it's a little sweeter than regular lime juice.

Makes approximately 32 ounces (945 milliliters)

Serves 10 to 16

PINK GRAPEFRUIT, THYME & CAVA

Zest from one pink grapefruit

2 1/2 cups (590 milliliters) freshly squeezed grapefruit juice

1 1/2 teaspoons (7 milliliters) citric acid*

1 chilled bottle Cava (750 milliliters / 25 ounces)

FOR THE THYME SYRUP

1 cup (235 milliliters) water

1 1/2 cups (300 grams) pure cane sugar

12 sprigs of fresh thyme

- - -

METHOD For the thyme syrup: Combine the water, sugar and thyme in a small saucepan. Bring to a boil and reduce to a simmer for 15 minutes. Remove from heat, put a lid on the pan and let steep for another 15 minutes. Strain the thyme syrup into a separate jar and let cool.

For the rest: Zest and juice your grapefruit and combine with the citric acid. Add 1 1/2 cups (355 milliliters) of the thyme syrup and combine. Immediately pour into a clean glass vessel and refrigerate.

TO SERVE Pour 1 to 2 ounces (30–60 milliliters) Cava into the bottom of your cup. Fill with shaved ice. Sculpt the top into a nice round shape. Drizzle 2–3 ounces (60–90 milliliters) of the pink grapefruit and thyme syrup over the top and finish with a sprig of fresh thyme.

*Citric acid can usually be found among the canning supplies at your local grocery store or in the spice aisle. If you can't find it, a healthy squeeze of fresh lemon juice is an excellent substitute.

Makes approximately 32 ounces (945 milliliters)

Serves 10 to 16

COCONUT & CARDAMOM

4 cups (945 milliliters) coconut juice*

2 cups (400 grams) pure cane sugar

2 tablespoons (30 milliliters) lemon juice

1/4 teaspoon ground cardamom

- - -

METHOD Mix all of the ingredients together until the sugar dissolves and the cardamom disperses.

TO SERVE Fill the cup with shaved ice. Sculpt the top into a nice round shape. Drizzle 2–3 ounces (60–90 milliliters) of the coconut and cardamom mixture over the top.

GARNISHES AND ADDITIONS If you want a stronger coconut flavor, you can sprinkle some dried coconut bits on top. Pistachios are also a beautiful and delicious garnish. And if you want the ultimate creamy coconut experience, a drizzle of sweetened condensed milk is a must. I learned about this from a friend who grew up in Japan and always enjoyed her snow cones this way as a little girl.

*I recommend Lakewood Organic Coconut Juice, which has a strong coconut flavor and a few all-natural thickeners, so the syrup ends up being nice and creamy.

Makes approximately 32 ounces (945 milliliters)

Serves 10 to 16 ○○

WHAT I LEARNED FROM THE SEA

AN INTERVIEW WITH MARK KURLANSKY BY KELSEY VALA

Working as a fisherman in his younger years, best-selling author Mark Kurlansky discovered that the sea gave him something to write about. Also the author of Salt: A World History, *he has plenty of wisdom to share about history, food, writing and life.*

Mark Kurlansky has had a ridiculous number of careers: food anthropologist, playwright, fisherman, dockworker, journalist, pastry chef, cook, paralegal, lecturer, teacher and author of more than 25 books, including *Salt: A World History*. We asked him a few questions about how the ocean helped shape his life, his writing and his career.

PLEASE TELL US ABOUT YOUR RELATIONSHIP WITH THE SEA.

I love to hear it, see the way light plays off of it, stand in it, run by it, swim in it, sail over it, be near it.

HOW DID YOUR TIME WORKING ON A COMMERCIAL FISHING BOAT INFLUENCE YOUR CAREER?

I first went to sea when I was 17 on a 45-foot wooden-hulled boat. I liked the camaraderie of belonging to a special group doing something unique. But more than anything I loved taking the boat out, piloting out of the harbor in purple morning light, picking up the spry and swells of the open sea just as the light heated to orange, and feeling that I was off to an adventure in the wild with the dull and predictable land disappearing behind me. I first did it because I thought it would inform my writing, but really it changed my life. It was a huge influence: the love of the sea, of fishing, of fishermen and fishing ports and an appreciation of hardworking people who yearn to be independent.

WHY DID YOU THINK YOUR TIME SPENT ON BOATS WOULD POSITIVELY AFFECT YOUR WRITING?

I just wanted to have life experiences. I imagined I'd write more specifically about it, but I went on to have other experiences. I decided I wanted to be a writer when I was eight years old and never wanted to do anything else. I see young writers who go to Ivy League colleges and make connections and have an agent on graduation and a book contract by the time they're 21 and show some facility with the craft of words. Great. But what are they going to write about? You have to go places and see things and have experiences to be a writer.

WHAT ARE SOME OF YOUR MOST VALUABLE MEMORIES OF THE SEA?

I often remember when I was lobstering in the trenches past New England and it would be so foggy that you literally couldn't see the bow from the stern of a 45-foot boat. These were some of the busiest lanes in the world heading into Long Island and then New York Harbor. We had no radio and no equipment of any kind; we even hauled by hand. I'd be hauling away and the fog would somehow seem darker, and then I'd hear this great deep sound and realize a freighter was bearing down on me. I'd quickly let go of the line or haul and grab this kazoo-like thing—our only horn—and start tooting while the captain ran for the wheel, pushed the throttle and managed to clear the giant's wake. It used to happen all the time. I learned that you're fearless when you're young, and the more you experience the less nerve you have. Life is dangerous and uncertain. You have to study up, be patient and know when to quit and when not to. Now there's an important skill.

YOU SAY PEOPLE HAVE COMPLEX RELATIONSHIPS WITH FOOD: HOW ABOUT YOURS?

I think of myself as a food anthropologist. I'm fascinated by what food tells us about ourselves and our society. I'm full of unanswered questions. Why did Ashkenazi Jewish women from Central Europe in the late 19th century use so much coconut? Why did New Yorkers start eating black and white cookies? I really want to know these things.

EVEN THOUGH YOU'VE WON NUMEROUS FOOD-WRITING AWARDS, YOU DON'T CONSIDER YOURSELF A FOOD WRITER. WHY IS THIS?

It's because I never write about food as food: It's always food as a way of seeing something else. I don't think half of my books are about food, but it's interesting that food so often shows up in my fiction. Maybe a good story needs some food? How else can you get to know the characters? I once wrote that I always hated being called a *gourmet*, but once the term *foodie* came along, gourmet didn't sound that bad.

WHAT MADE YOU WANT TO WRITE CHILDREN'S BOOKS ON SERIOUS SUBJECTS SUCH AS WAR, SALT AND ENVIRONMENTAL SEA ISSUES?

Children are ideal readers. They are very curious and they haven't made up their minds about anything. So it's fun to write for them. Besides, how else can you try to make the world better?

DO YOU CONSIDER YOURSELF AN ENVIRONMENTALIST?

Yes, but I have a lot of issues with my fellow environmentalists. I find a lot of them to be self-righteous and arrogant classists who have no respect for or understanding of working people. They lecture us about food, land use, pesticides, genetically modified organisms, local farming and organic food, but they never talk to farmers. They know all about the faults of commercial fishing, but they've never been to sea; they know nothing about how to fish and have never spoken to fishermen. They tell us all about how to make food that's good for the environment but so expensive that most people can't afford it. There are exceptions, of course.

HOW HAS FISHING CHANGED OVER TIME?

Commercial fishing is completely different today. You don't feel independent, you have a list of things you can and can't do and you spend more time thinking about how to deal with regulations than thinking about finding fish. When I started we talked a lot about tides, weather conditions and trends. Today everyone is talking about regulations, which *are* necessary: Someone has to keep an eye on things and make decisions, and that needs to be done with an overview, not just the microcosm of individual boats or even fleets. In fact, it should be even broader than it is. Instead of trying to manage fish stocks, they should be trying to manage ecosystems. Regulations should acknowledge that everything impacts everything else.

DO FISHERMEN STILL NEED TO UNDERSTAND TIDES AND WEATHER TO BE SUCCESSFUL?

Tides determine life cycles of fish. If you don't know the tides, you can't find the fish. They also sometimes control the use of gear. For example, you can only haul lobster pots in slack tides because the buoys will be unseen under the water in a fast moving tide. Temperature also has a major impact on the life cycle of fish, which is one of several reasons why climate change is playing havoc with commercial fishing.

WHAT HAS THE SEA TAUGHT YOU ABOUT YOUR PLACE IN THE WORLD?

It teaches you that you're supposed to be on the land. Everything else is a crazy dare. ○ ○

NAUTICAL INK

We plunge seaward to dig up the meanings behind these classic maritime tattoos.

WORDS BY NIKAELA MARIE PETERS & ILLUSTRATIONS BY KAYE BLEGVAD

Tattoos have their roots in the sea. The widespread popularity of inking skin today could be credited to Captain James Cook, who introduced a tattooed Polynesian man to the English court in the late 1700s: Sailors have been returning home with tattoos ever since.

Sailors have always been superstitious and tattoos acted as luck charms and talismans. For example, an image of a star or compass was said to guide you home, or "hold fast" written on the knuckles supposedly enhanced a sailor's grip. Tattoos told stories, recorded accomplishments and declared prayers and affections. They marked the passage of time. They made public what would have otherwise been private: homesickness and hope. They also acted as a type of uniform,

displaying the rank and role of a seaman: a rope around the wrist for a deckhand, a harpoon for a member of a fishing fleet.

There must have been something comforting about the uniformity of these symbols. It was a language you learned rather than invented. Tattoos delineated communities and marked family members. Each symbol carried significant tradition and history. Perhaps what makes tattoos so interesting today is that throughout most of history they've been both traditional practice and countercultural defiance—both a way of blending in and a unique mark of self-expression. But for sailors in the 1800s, tattoos were commonplace, an unquestioned part of the uniform.

SHIP AT FULL MAST This beautiful tattoo denoted a sailor who had been around the edge of Cape Horn, the notorious southernmost point in Chile. It's a wayfarer's tattoo: The image evokes notions of the wind, the waves and the wandering to this day.

ANCHOR A single anchor signified that a sailor had crossed the Atlantic or had been part of the Merchant Marines. Two anchors crossed over one another was a sign of a senior crewman, responsible for the hull of the boat. The metaphor is also clear: It symbolizes all that grounds and is steadfast.

GOLDEN DRAGON A golden dragon tattoo was another image denoting accomplishment: It showed that a sailor had crossed the International Date Line or had been to Asia. It's also the Chinese symbol of strength and luck.

SWALLOW This was a visual reminder of one's ability to survive, noting that a sailor had sailed 5,000 nautical miles. It was also a symbol of return or a safe journey back to land: Swallows' migration patterns are consistent, so they always return "home." Also, spotting a swallow while out at sea told a sailor land was nearby.

MERMAID The image of a woman, half-human half-fish, is a newer tattoo, not popular with sailors until the 1900s. It may have symbolized followed dreams. It may have symbolized seduction. The mythical creature also has ties to Roman and Greek creation stories, so her image may have also suggested creativity.

SHELLBACK TURTLE The turtle (though sometimes represented as King Neptune) signified that a sailor had traveled across the equator. It was worn as a badge of honor or a souvenir, like a tack pinned into a map telling strangers where you'd been.

HARPOON An image of this brutal yet effective tool came to symbolize a member of a fishing fleet. Although out of general use by the 1800s, the harpoon retained the symbolism of a fisherman.

THE PIG AND ROOSTER This pair of lucky charm tattoos was believed to prevent drowning. Sailors wore the rooster on their right foot and the pig on their left. These two animals were rumored to be the only survivors of shipwrecks; the buoyant crates they were kept in acted as lifeboats. ○ ○

PHOTO ESSAY

THE SALT FLATS OF BOLIVIA

*Dutch photographer Scarlett Hooft Graafland has been traveling to
Bolivia's Salar de Uyuni salt flats for more than a decade. By placing
unexpected objects in these panoramas, she draws attention to the
surreal beauty of the land and the incongruous nature of life there.*

WORDS BY GEORGIA FRANCES KING & PHOTOGRAPHS BY SCARLETT HOOFT GRAAFLAND

WHAT INTERESTED YOU IN PHOTOGRAPHING BOLIVIA'S SALT FLATS?

It's amazing to be in a place where all you can see is whiteness: No sounds, almost no life, just white salt everywhere you can see. Some are plain white areas, some have patterns made by the wind on the ground and then there are a few tiny islands in the middle of the desert with cacti that are hundreds of years old. And sometimes, in the beginning of March, there's a thin layer of water on top of the salt that turns the desert into one big mirror.

HOW DO YOU CONCEPTUALIZE YOUR IDEAS? WHAT DO OBJECTS LIKE THE COTTON CANDY SYMBOLIZE?

For "Sweating Sweethearts," a portrait series of local women in the Salar, I wanted to make a monument to them and have them sit on piles of salt like a pedestal. It's all about sweet versus salty: the sweet cotton candy with the stark landscape, the strong round candy shape with the triangular salt pile shape, the bright pink color with their local skirts and old-fashioned hats... It's also some kind of celebration. These women are in a tough position, and this is my way to give them some respect.

WHAT PLACE DO THE SALT FLATS HAVE IN BOLIVIAN CULTURE?

For local people, the Salar is something like a holy place. When you enter, you have to pay tribute to the god of the desert, put some coca leaves and alcohol on the tires of your car and say some prayers in order to have a safe trip. It's so huge that it can actually be a dangerous place. When you get lost, it could take days before someone will find you. There are many casualties in the Salar.

WHAT KIND OF MESSAGE ARE YOU TRYING TO SEND WITH YOUR PHOTOGRAPHS OF BOLIVIA?

It's a celebration of the beauty of nature. Like the way the wind produces those hexagonal patterns on the ground: I filled those shapes with powders and spices from the local market to emphasize "nature-made design." I love to play with that notion. Maybe it's because I come from the Netherlands where there is no wilderness at all. Everything we have there is man-made design. I long for places where you can strongly feel the power of nature. The landscape seems to almost dictate the outcome of my photographs.

HOW DID YOU CONNECT WITH THE LOCALS IN BOLIVIA?

I was lucky to meet Bolivian installation artist Gastón Ugalde, who was once called "the Andy Warhol of the Andes" by *The New York Times.* So with him and his crew—and with the help of the local people of Uyuni, the town near the desert—we were able to get a lot of things done. The help and goodwill of the local community is an important element in my work, though it isn't always visible.

YOU SHOOT USING ANALOG CAMERAS AND DON'T USE PHOTOSHOP: WHY DO YOU PREFER TO ESCHEW MODERN METHODS?

I just love the deep colors of the analog photos—it's hard to beat that. I like that there's no manipulation done in the photos whatsoever. The fact that I print the photo right from the negative is part of my work: What you see is what you get. ○ ○

For more about Scarlett's work, visit Michael Hoppen Contemporary in London (michaelhoppengallery.com).

THE SQUID FISHER'S HANDBOOK

How much fresher can dinner get than a squid pulled directly from the sea and put into your mouth? Photographer James Bowden offers expert advice on ways to catch and eat squid.

PHOTOGRAPHS BY JAMES BOWDEN

HOW HARD IS IT TO CATCH A SQUID?

Squid can be tricky to catch, but once you've got the hang of it they're so much fun and hugely addictive. The most important thing is location. Pontoons or jetties are ideal as they usually have lights on them that attract squid in the fading light of the evening, which is the best time to try fishing for them. Look for somewhere not too deep with reef or seagrass beds below for the squid to hide among. If you see a jetty with black ink stains on the top, you know it's a good spot where squid are caught. You use a rod, a reel and a squid jig (a small prawn-shaped lure with loads of spikes at the end) to snag the squid when they attack. It can be extremely frustrating as squid can be very picky about the color of the lure and the time of day! You cast the jig and reel it in, jerking the line to best imitate a swimming prawn. When they hopefully strike, keep the tension on the line so they can't thrust back off the hooks, and then reel them in steadily and slowly, watching out for the inevitable jettison of ink!

WHAT KIND OF GEAR DO WE NEED TO SQUID FISH?

A rod and reel, a collection of different colored squid jigs and, as with most fishing, a fair bit of patience. Luckily the best time to catch squid is on really calm, warm summer evenings, so it's generally always a beautiful time to be hanging out down by the ocean.

DO THEY REALLY SPRAY THAT MUCH INK AT YOU?

Oh yeah! As soon as they're snagged on the lure, they will begin to spray their ink. You can try and aim the imminent spray away from you by keeping the tension on the line as you pull them in. But, in the excitement of it all, you'll probably forget this and it's likely you or someone nearby will get sprayed! My girlfriend rarely comes squid fishing with me anymore as I generally always seem to get her covered with ink. It's a nightmare to get off clothing, so don't wear your Sunday best fishing.

WHAT'S YOUR FAVORITE WAY TO PREPARE THEM?

Preparing them is really easy. You can gut and clean them on the dock using just your hands. The best parts to eat are the body tube, tentacles and wings (the body and wings need to be skinned first). Best to avoid the head, cartilage and guts, though you can keep the ink sac from the guts to make black pasta sauce.

My favorite recipe is bread-crumbed calamari: Simply clean, dry and slice the body into rings. Dust the rings with flour, dip in egg white and cover with panko breadcrumbs. Then fry in 1 to 2 centimeters of really hot oil until they're light brown on both sides. Drain the oil and serve with a chunk of lemon… so so good!

SQUID CLEANING TIPS:

+ Start by dislocating the head and tentacles from the body with a quick pull.
+ Keep the tentacles by cutting them from the head and discard the rest.
+ Pick up the body and pull out the guts and ink sac using your fingers.
+ Feel around till you find the cartilage (called "the pen") and pull it out too.
+ Peel the wing-like parts from the body, then skin both the wings and the main body tube.
+ Wash thoroughly with water. ○ ○

James Bowden is a freelance photographer based either on the south coast of England or in Hobart, Tasmania.

LIFE ON THE WATER

*What's it like to spend every day in, on or next to the water?
We visited four families in Italy, Denmark, New Zealand and Maine
to find out what life is like when the sea is just outside your door.*

A GREEK VILLA IN ITALY *Polignano a Mare, Italy*

While traveling through Italy in the late '80s, Danish couple Lars and Pernille Lembcke's hunt for tasty produce led them to Puglia, the heel of the country's boot. Twenty years later they had the chance to purchase an ancient stone home there in the seaside town of Polignano a Mare, which looks out across the Adriatic Sea. "We were a young couple in love, and we fell in love with this place!" she says. The town was settled by the Greeks around 500 B.C. and the house had stood abandoned for 15 years when they bought it. Most of the structure was built out of the stones from the cliff face it sits in, including stairs cut out of solid rock. In the not-so-distant past, the previous owners had used the ground floor to keep their livestock and even had a donkey turning a shredder to grind grains on the terrace. That room has now been converted into their kitchen, and where their bedroom now stands was once the stables. "From the outside it just looks like a normal town house, but as soon as you enter you are dragged by the light to the sea-facing kitchen and out onto the large terrace courtyard that hangs 20 meters above the

water," she says. "The first and last thing we do every day is inhale the sea. The main bedroom is facing it, so the first thing we experience in the morning is the big blue." Pernille enjoys running along the stone wall that faces Croatia and Montenegro, whereas her husband prefers taking swims in the cool water with Guido, the local poet, who is a member of their "community of bon vivants." During the summer, the locals congregate on the streets for impromptu standing picnics where they celebrate the glut of the season. "It's always very relaxed with no stress or fuss about the cooking," she says, "It's not about showing off—it's about the food and having fun together." Hosting a luncheon means half the town could show up on your stoop, but as long as they bring some extra food, she doesn't mind. Fresh produce plays a huge part of daily life, and many of the town's inhabitants like to swap groceries instead of using money. Pernille's neighbors own a fish shop, and the wife claims she never has to buy food because she can trade her husband's fish for everything she wants. "Even though people might not have a lot of

money, they never compromise when it comes to food," she says. And what more could you ask for when you live in such idyllic surroundings? With the sea at your feet and fresh produce in the farms, every day is as pleasant as the next. They wake up to the gentle talk of the fishermen emptying their nets every morning, especially when the sea is calm. "We get up, open the shutters and are overwhelmed by the golden morning light and the reflections off the sea. As soon as we're up and dressed, then it's time to face the street life on the other side of the house with the neighbors doing their morning routines," she says. There is no doubt that life by the sea has a healing quality, and Pernille's recent life experiences are a testament to that. After she was diagnosed with breast cancer three years ago, she believes her proximity to the ocean has helped improve her state of mind. "Of course it was a devastating experience, but I'm quite sure that what made me go through the treatment and recovery quite easily (in addition to incredible support from my husband and family) was a combination of meditation and staying by the sea as much as possible," she says. "In a painful life crisis, the awareness of being a small, almost insignificant part of the universe supplies a lot of renewed energy and courage. It made me aware of what really matters in life and what I can do to sustain these values." ○ ○

Photographs by Wichmann + Bendtsen &
Styling by Helle Walsted

SLIDING DOORS *Sjælland's Western Coast, Denmark*

"My favorite part is being outside, even when we are inside," says Lene Tranberg, referring to the modest geometric home she, her husband and her son share on the western coast of Sjælland. Made with wood and metal, the structure's sloping triangular roof gives way to wide windows that create very little differentiation between the sand, the sea and their living room. The family chose to live by the sea so they could "feel the vibrations and ever-changing atmosphere" of the water. These feelings are enhanced by the fact that many of the walls of their home sit on sliding doors, opening the house up to the impulse of the elements. The slightest change in weather makes a huge difference to the light that streams into the house and the types of days that can be enjoyed: canoeing and kayaking on calm mornings, reading in the rooftop alcoves on chilly afternoons and watching the rain stream down the windows from the kitchen when it's drizzly. Out of all the weather patterns, it's the inevitable wind that accompanies coastal lifestyles that Lene's still trying to learn to love. But it's what she calls "the character of the elements" that also attracts her most to this little plot of land. The original homes built in this quaint countryside were once used as the beach houses for local farmers. It's a location rich with history—which Lene says rests in ancient Viking land—with many families having lived here for generations. This made her household a rare new addition to the town when a local craftsman built it for them five years ago. As an architect, she enjoys the simplicity of her home and the ability to "see the open horizons" from most vantage points. And with views like these, why would you ever want to return to landlocked life? ○ ○

Photographs by Wichmann + Bendtsen & Styling by Helle Walsted

THE CLIFF-TOP STUDIO *Anawhata Beach, New Zealand*

"There's daily drama when you live by the water, and just how epic that drama is has become more obvious to me as I spend time away from it," says Judy Millar, a visual artist and New Zealand native. "When I travel, I carry the image of the sea with me." Thirty years ago Judy visited the perilous coastline of Anawhata Beach, an hour west of Auckland, and immediately felt at home. She started talking to the locals and found someone willing to give up four acres of their land for a tiny sum of money. Once she had secured her view, she set about sourcing building materials from construction sites by swapping crates of beer for wood and glass. "I've learned an amazing amount about building for coastal conditions," she says. "In New Zealand, rain can be driven horizontally by the wind, so the normal ways to make a house watertight needed to be completely rethought." Thanks to a recently graduated architect friend, she constructed her home from scratch. It's completely off the grid, so she relies on solar power and pumping water to get by, living at the mercy of the weather's whims. The house sits high above the water with the light of the ocean constantly bouncing off different walls, and her studio is a sunlit space where the salty air and her paint tubes mingle. "The influence of the landscape and surroundings on my work is difficult to pinpoint, but breadth, scale, drama, color and spectacle have all taken increasingly important roles," she says. Her art has taken her to bodies of water and land around the world, including representing New Zealand at the Venice Biennale in 2009. She now splits her time between her self-made home in Auckland and a studio in Berlin. "I grew up very close to a beach," she says. "The sea was always there, not taken for granted, but part of life: Tides, storms and light on the water were always part of my world. The relationship of land and sea was seamless." Many Kiwis share this deep connection with the sea that's imbued in them from childhood. Judy believes that being surrounded at all edges by huge masses of water has made them a curious culture. "People constantly look out to sea and wonder what's going on across the water," she says. "We have a strong desire to travel but also a great sense of independence and resolve. Living surrounded by the sea has shaped us as a people in many ways." ○ ○

Photographs by Shantanu Starick

ON THE ROCKS *Brooklin, Maine*

Faith Field has visited the Maine holiday home her family built by hand for the past 75 summers, one for every year of her life. Her father constructed this oceanside house of granite and wood in 1937, and Faith was brought into the world two years later. The rocky shores of the small fishing town of Brooklin, Maine, became the backdrop for many of her formative years and have continued to influence her as the decades go on. "Getting on a boat and going off for a sail is something I've done all my life," she says. "I just love being by the water." Faith taught herself how to sail while at several childhood summer camps in Massachusetts and honed her craft on her father's boat off the coast of Brooklin. That same 12-and-a-half-foot sailboat is still moored on their dock, along with a newer vessel that she takes out regularly on her warm-weather jaunts. Nestled between towering evergreen trees on a rocky ledge, her summer property is equal parts portentous lighthouse and Norwegian gingerbread house. "The place was something that came out of the architect and my father's mind, and I wish I could have been there as a fly on the wall to listen as they created this place," she says.

"I don't know how they thought it up, but they did." All the windows open up to the sea, and there are plenty of nooks to sit and read while watching the crabbing boats drift by. According to Faith, the secluded positioning of the community—"it's off the beaten track, so to speak"—has meant that the area and its people haven't changed all that much over the past three quarters of a century: They're still fishermen, lobsterers and boat builders. "Good, solid, hardworking, honest people," Faith says. "They're the salt of the earth." Many of the vacationers like Faith that spent a lifetime of summers visiting have now moved there permanently and have become locals. "I've spent every summer of my life on the water, and both my husband, Peder, and I love the ocean and love to sail," she says. "If you're talking to me, I would've moved here a long time ago!" The couple owns an apple orchard in inland Massachusetts that keeps them from living in Maine full time. When they were newly married, it was simply too expensive to buy a house of their own by the ocean. Instead, they purchased the orchard in 1962 and still run it themselves, but that doesn't stop Faith's summers. "If we

moved to Maine, Peder would wonder how he'd spend his time," she says. "He loves taking care of his apple trees." When not tending to his crops, he can be coaxed into immersing himself in the cold, coastal waters for swims, but Faith prefers taking the boats out for a drift. She and one of her four sisters inherited the property, and though her sister has now passed, her family and Faith's alternate their summer trips there. "About a year and a half ago, we started a fourth generation with a great-granddaughter," Faith says, "so the family's thought is that we'll keep it going for as long as we can." ○ ○

Photographs by Shantanu Starick

FEW

ENTERTAINING FOR A FEW

○ ○ ○

PHOTO ESSAY

TURNING POINT: A GUIDE TO FLIPPING

*What does it feel like to fly? We headed to Crystal Palace
in Southeast London to have the girls show us how it's done.*

PHOTOGRAPHS BY MARK SANDERS

BASIC TIPS Judges look for how little splash you make on entering, how tightly your legs are squeezed together, the arc of your arms and the straightness of your body. Don't flip off safety, either: Remember to jump as far away from the edge as possible—whether it's a cliff or a springboard— and always check the depth of the water you're diving into. Flips are no fun if the ambulance has to cut short your display of airborne finesse.

THE DOUBLE CANNONBALL This is the only dive (if you can even call it that) where your splash should be optimal. It's also a maneuver that has the best visual effect in twos. Synchronize your leap with your partner by tucking in your knees and pointing your toes. Also called "The Bomb," it has the ability to cause catastrophic water destruction to everything nearby. It's mandatory that you scream this dive's name as you plunge into the water.

THE GAINER This flip isn't recommended for those who are faint of heart (or sensitive of skin). The main rule for a Gainer is to get as much forward velocity as possible so you don't end up cracking your skull on your jumping platform. Take a running start, project yourself both toward the middle of the water and as high as you can, spin your legs backward over your head and desperately try not to suffer a totally debilitating spinal injury.

THE SWAN One of the simplest dives, the Swan is also the hardest to perfect. Raise your arms above your head as you come off the springboard while arching your back and looking up, then slowly bring your fingers together as you reach the surface of the water, entering with your hands. It's very easy for this to turn into the Ugly Duckling dive if not executed properly, but it could someday become beautiful with a little practice.

THE BACKWARD ONE-AND-A-HALF-TWIST
ARM-STAND DOUBLE SOMERSAULT PIKE
SOMETHING-SOMETHING
You're on your own.

THE CHANGING STATE OF THE SEA

PHOTOGRAPHS BY TEC PETAJA (PAGE 118) & BOBBY MILLS (PAGE 121)

*We asked a few folks—including a marine biologist,
a sustainable fisherman and a free diver—to recount what
they've witnessed and what the sea means to them.*

ERIC FLEMING: surfer, artist, teacher (Olympia, Washington)

ERIKA GREBELDINGER: marine biologist (Vancouver Island, BC)

BEN JACOBSEN: founder, Jacobsen Salt Co. (Portland and Netarts, Oregon)

MARK BITTERMAN: author of *Salted* and owner of the Meadow (Portland, Oregon, and New York)

KIRK LOMBARD: sustainable fishmonger, Sea Forager Seafood (San Francisco, California)

MARCUS MØLLER BITSCH: photographer, free diver, surfer (Aarhus, Denmark)

WHAT IS YOUR RELATIONSHIP WITH THE SEA?

Eric: The sea and me get along wonderfully together. The ocean gives me peace, adventure, a sense of wonder, thrills and puzzles, and I give back a careful way of life that minimizes my contribution to rising sea levels and pollution. I feel like the ocean gives me much more than I give back. If you have a chance to be at, on or in the ocean, always take it.

Erika: One of respect. I have a strong passion, curiosity and amazement for it and all the creatures that thrive in it. The ocean is powerful and not a force to be reckoned with.

Ben: My relationship with the sea is close: I watch it closely each day—the salinity, the river runoff, the turbidity and the calmness of it.

Mark: Submergence is my preferred state. I grew up in Santa Barbara, so the sea was my front yard and I was more or less a semi-aquatic mammal, always bodysurfing, sailing and lots and lots of swimming.

Marcus: As a kid I wanted to be an astronaut but quickly realized only a few have the chance to be weightless, so I chose the second best: free diving. I started buying disposable underwater cameras on vacations to show my family what an amazing world I witnessed, and that's how my passion for photography started.

Kirk: I teach people how to forage the Pacific shores. I provide sustainable seafood to "seafoodetarians" who care about the oceans.

HOW HAS THE SEA INFLUENCED YOU AS A PERSON?

Mark: There are two kinds of people: outer space people and ocean people. One fantasizes about the impossible enormity of the celestial void, the other of the aquatic depths. I was always an ocean person. Walking the beach at dawn and finding a buoy from the Philippines is a gift from nature every bit as miraculous as a meteorite. The sea has helped me to understand the vast interconnected diversity of our planet and inspired me to explore it.

Eric: Spending a lot of time in the ocean has given me greater courage and resilience, and made me more patient and compassionate. It's also ruined me forever from spending much time inland: If I'm away from the sea for too long, I get the heebie-jeebies.

Erika: When I'm on, in and around the ocean, I'm calm. The ocean gives me clarity. There's no place I'd rather be.

Ben: It's humbling, for sure. It's just so powerful, and we're such tiny blips on the earth. It's easy to take it for granted, but it's also something that you never forget.

Marcus: The sea has this indescribable peacefulness to it and yet a majestic power. It calms me down like nothing else. It's been my hiding spot when my surroundings have been too stressful. You're alone with your senses and the surrounding nature. All stress and worries disappear for a matter of time and you feel a beautiful silentness.

WHAT KINDS OF THINGS HAVE YOU SEEN FLOATING AROUND IN THE OCEAN?

Kirk: I recently found a 9mm handgun while clamming.

Mark: I've seen a dock that washed over from Japan after the tsunami hit, and I've seen waves of bioluminescent plankton.

Erika: Much of marine life started as tiny plankton, so there's always something cruising by. On one occasion I saw a baby octopus that was mostly transparent except for small colorful speckles. The speckles were the start of chromatophores, the color pigments that give octopods the ability to change their skin color to match their surroundings. We stared at each other for a brief moment before it drifted by.

Eric: At one of my favorite surf spots in the Strait of Juan de Fuca, there is always a river otter floating around. He is cute, drifting around on his back until you get too close to him, then he hisses like a cat and bares his teeth. He's got spirit!

Marcus: Our seas are getting more and more damaged and polluted. I've seen everything from dolls floating around to old guns to big car parts. Unfortunately you'll be able to find something almost everywhere. Even in the most isolated places, you will occasionally see small plastic parts floating around on the oceans's surface.

HOW HAS THE SEA CHANGED OVER TIME AND WHAT CAN BE DONE TO SLOW THESE CHANGES?

Eric: Education is a powerful tool: If people are aware of their impacts, they may be more inclined to help lessen them. When we feel an inherent connection to something, we're more likely to want to protect it.

Ben: Increased pH levels and the resulting acidity have had a really tough impact on shell fishermen. I have many friends who are oyster farmers and shellfish hatchery owners and they're having a difficult time with it. The consensus is that hatchery days are limited until they can figure out a permanent solution.

Mark: We're dependent on the sea in ways we don't even fully understand until something wakes us up to it. The tsunami that hit Japan and the threat of radiation scared off the whole subject of Japanese salt, despite the fact that the currents and prevailing winds spared the vast majority of salt makers from any radiation.

Kirk: The sea changes. Why do people assume that these changes are always bad? The sea and the creatures in it are in a constant state of flux. Obviously things like oil spills, accumulation of industrial wastes and Fukushima are terrible, but many other supposedly calamitous changes are natural cycles: Things like the constant cycles of abundance and decline in fish stocks are not always due to human influences. Often they are, but not always. It's good to remember this before hitting the collective panic button.

HOW CAN WE HELP?

Erika: Lessen your impact on our environment by reducing your wastes and carbon footprint: recycle, compost, buy only what you need and get outside and enjoy the outdoors! When you are out and about, do your part and pick up garbage that you see—it could save an animal's life.

Eric: A few simple things you can do now are to stop using pesticides, herbicides and fungicides, limit your driving and find ways to reduce the amount of plastic you contribute to landfills. Water eventually takes most things to the sea and an ocean full of substances such as motor oil, chunks of plastic and emission particles that kill bugs, plants, fungus and algae makes an unpleasant environment for everyone.

Mark: The easiest and most delicious way I can think of is to buy the right salt. Don't buy the industrial sea salt in a cheap tube at the supermarket: That's made in ponds, and they generally wipe out more wetlands than they help to preserve, have all the sea's natural minerals stripped out and are tended by diesel-belching excavators. Buy natural, hand-harvested sea salt that's made using the 100 percent renewable energy of the sun.

Kirk: If people really want to help the oceans, they need to stop eating so many of the "Apex predator fish" such as tunas, swordfish, sea bass and halibut. If health and sustainability are the goals, we should consider eating a few sardines, anchovies or herring every now and then. They don't bioaccumulate heavy metals and other toxins the way tuna does. They're tasty and their stocks are able to rebound much faster than slower-growing predatory fish. Okay, I'm off my soapbox.

WHAT'S YOUR FAVORITE FISHERMAN'S TALE?

Eric: I once went deep-sea fishing and noticed that there were no life jackets or lifeboats on board. I asked the first mate, "Say, I notice there's nothing to save us in the event of an accident. What happens if we sink?" and the dude replied, "It's farther than I can swim and more water than I can drink, so it looks like I'm going to drown."

Erika: My friend and I were scuba diving in a sheltered bay in Bamfield, British Columbia. Mysids [krill-like organisms] are a favorite food of gray whales and were throughout the water column that day. We were 30 feet below the surface when the water around us went dark. Two gray whales were also in the bay and decided to feed right above us. We finished our dive, sat on the sandy beach and enjoyed the feeding frenzy as the gray whales lunged and splashed in the emerald ocean.

Mark: Last summer we set sail from Portsmouth, England, for Split, Croatia, and headed straight into a gale that lasted three weeks. It was the shittiest experience ever in so many ways, yet definitely one of the wildest, most beautiful and fun experiences of my life: stars so low and heavy they made you flinch, dolphins playing like Labradors off the bow, danger enveloped in crushing beauty, being clipped onto the jack lines in seas churned by 40-knot winds at 3 a.m. with a lover pressed next to me, drinking sweet tea. As we got farther south and the rains let up a bit, salt took over everything: the ropes, the bunks, my clothes and my beard, and salt became the flavor of everything my lips touched. ○ ○ ○

THE CASE FOR CRYING

WORDS BY ROMY ASH & PHOTOGRAPH BY ANJA VERDUGO

Salty tears have a communicative power beyond words and reason.
But what happens when the waterworks are nothing but crocodile tears,
caused by exhaustion, frustration or even a stubborn onion?

In Roman times, when their husbands went to sea, sailors' wives used to keep "tear bottles" to capture their watery woe. When the sailors returned, they could literally measure how much their wives had really missed them: It was a pretty, albeit controlling, idea. But what was to stop the women from filling the jar with the seawater their loves had sailed away on? It's as salty as tears, and it would certainly withstand a taste test.

People don't have to be sad to cry. If I'd been a Roman sailor's wife, it would've been an easy deceit: When I'm tired, I can cry enough to fill a whole tear bottle without the slightest tinge of sadness. After all, tears can express the whole gamut of human emotion, and most of them don't deal with despair: They can represent ecstasy and joy right across the spectrum to fear, frustration, shock, powerlessness, anger and empathy. But it's exhaustion that brings me to tears.

Weeping when you're emotional releases a concoction of hormones that act as a liquid painkiller to calm your mood. All of the other varieties—the reflexive tears that well when cutting onions, or the basal type you produce all day to keep your eyes clean—are essentially crocodile tears, appearing without emotion. Crying could happen at any moment, for any reason, or even no reason at all. It requires a lot of explaining.

"Tears, idle tears, I know not what they mean"

— ALFRED LORD TENNYSON

Consider this: I'm waiting at a stopover, midway through a long-haul flight to Europe, which from my home in the Southern Hemisphere takes a mere 24 hours. I have no idea what time it actually is, just that I'm bone tired. As we take off, I begin to cry. They are tired tears, but the woman sitting next to me pats my arm, gives me a tissue and tells me everything is going to be all right. When the seat belt sign turns off, the flight attendant notices me, crouches down and sighs, "Boys. I'm so sorry, love." I leave it a moment too late to correct her mistake and spend the flight living out this false story, simultaneously hoping for an upgrade and feeling deep shame at my unintended sham.

The sympathetic flight attendant was responding to the communicative power of my tears. Little did she realize that the real message my tears were sending was *go to sleep*. Thomas Dixon, director of the Queen Mary Centre for the History of Emotions (yes, there is such a center), says there's a communicative power to weeping: It's part of language. When we cry, we are asking for help without words, or letting those around us know we're experiencing any one of a scope of deep emotions.

If there's one thing I've learned from my spontaneous bouts of tears, it is that it's okay to cry. It's even acceptable to cry in public. I've gotten better at explaining my tears, and sometimes I ignore their message to *go to sleep* and keep dancing, eating, talking. With a wet, salty face, I keep on. ○ ○ ○

When Romy Ash isn't writing about food, she writes fiction. Her debut novel, Floundering, *isn't a gourmet book: The characters only consume fish and chips, ice cream and soda. She lives in Melbourne, Australia.*

PERU'S SALTED PONDS

WORDS BY GEORGIA FRANCES KING & PHOTOGRAPHS BY JAMES CHOROROS

James Chororos spent his honeymoon hiking, exploring and photographing Peru, including the pre-Inca salt pools near the valley town of Maras. He takes us along on his journey through the mountains.

Nestled between the altitude sickness–inducing mountains in Peru's central south are the Salineras de Maras, translating to the salt ponds of Maras. These evaporation pools climb up the hillside and number into the hundreds. Predating the Incas, they're believed to have been built by the Chanapata people sometime between 200 and 900 A.D. New York photographer James Chororos and his wife sought out these remote agricultural wonders on their travels.

CAN YOU PLEASE GIVE US A BRIEF RUNDOWN ON YOUR TRAVELS THROUGH PERU?

My wife and I are both pretty adventurous, so when we began planning our honeymoon, we decided early on to forgo cocktails on the beach in favor of outdoor exploration and camping. Less than 24 hours after our wedding, we boarded a flight from New York City to Peru. Our first days were spent getting accustomed to Inca history and making the rounds through many of the popular historical sites. We even had a beautiful and traditional Inca wedding ceremony, produced by a Q'ero elder and a few locals! That was a pretty rad experience. The pace from then on was quite different though. Each day we visited at least one new location and spent the entire day hiking and exploring. At night we camped or crashed in a hostel for a few hours before doing it all over again. The amount of hiking we did helped us acclimate to the high altitude in preparation for the four-day trek on the Inca Trail, which ends at Machu Picchu.

HOW DOES THE SALINERAS DE MARAS COMMUNITY OPERATE?

Most families in the area own a few ponds that have been passed down to them: They harvest the salt from their pools to sell in the markets. There's a high-salinity stream of water that flows into each one around the perimeter of the mines. Thick layers of salt eventually begin forming around the perimeter and bottom of them. When a pool is ready to be harvested, it's cut off from the water source with a stone and the water sitting inside it is left to evaporate. The harvester then extracts the salt crystals that formed in the pool as fresh salt.

WHAT DOES THE SURROUNDING AREA LOOK LIKE?

There isn't much development at the salt mines, or anywhere in Maras: just a ton of open, mountainous land. It was the most beautiful region we visited by far. There's so much untouched land out there and it's all super quiet and abnormally beautiful. We took a taxi on a miniature road trip from the village of Písac. The only way to approach the salt ponds is from the peak of the valley they're nestled in via a narrow and winding dirt road. When viewing the ponds from the entrance road, it's very hard to tell what you're looking at. They're beautiful but incredibly abstract, so you get almost no sense of the scale until you're out there standing on one.

WHAT EFFECT HAS YOUR EXPERIENCE IN MARAS HAD ON YOU?

The time I spent there changed my perspective on my current lifestyle in New York City, for sure. I couldn't help but think about the fact that I would soon be returning to one of the most densely developed landmasses on the planet. With that in mind, I took my time in Maras to zen out and enjoy the landscape. You truly feel like you're on another planet entirely. The geological formations, the dynamic sky and the absence of almost all audible noise make it feel very alien. No photograph can express the feeling of being there.

HOW DID PERU FEEL DIFFERENT TO OTHER PLACES YOU HAVE ADVENTURED?

The amount of completely undeveloped land in Peru is impressive, and the deep spiritual connection the natives have with the mountains and valleys is unlike anything I've experienced elsewhere. One thing about Peru that will always stay with me is how incredible the atmosphere is. The sky can change your mood by the hour and each phase is more beautiful than the last.

WHAT WERE THE PEOPLE YOU ENCOUNTERED LIKE?

We didn't meet a single Peruvian we didn't like. Everyone was very helpful, welcoming and informative. The inhabitants of the Sacred Valley all live so simply it's almost like you went back in time. Many make their own clothes, build their own homes, walk many miles to their destinations and are deeply rooted in Inca tradition.

WHAT'S ONE OF YOUR FAVORITE STORIES FROM YOUR TIME THERE?

It happened on a photo walk along a back trail near Písac. At one point I noticed a man jogging toward me holding a large wooden pole with an arched metal blade at the end—basically the grim reaper. He was approaching pretty quickly so I nervously grabbed a tripod from my pack, extended the legs and prepared to defend myself. When he was about 10 feet away, he stopped, smiled and said "*Eres un fotografo!*" which means, "You're a photographer!" He had noticed my gear and had a question about an old camera he owns. We chatted for a bit and ultimately I felt safe enough to ask him about his weapon. He laughed and explained it was an agricultural scythe: He was on his way to a farm where he harvests crops. I felt pretty stupid, but in the end it was a funny way to make a new friend and reversed any fear I had about exploring the area.

WHEN DID YOU PICK UP AN INTEREST IN PHOTOGRAPHY?

It began when I was a freshman in art school, but as I got deeper into school I became increasingly more fearful of pursuing art as a career. I worked as an architect for years before confirming that I was never meant for an office job. I wasn't creating enough as an architect, so I started shooting again. After a few months of burning the candle at both ends, I left architecture to become a full-time photographer. When I'm out photographing or even editing work, I've found that it's the only time I'm truly not thinking about anything else. When a shoot wraps up or I finish an edit, I have to take a few moments and re-engage myself into reality. It's become the best form of meditation for me. ○ ○ ○

James Chororos is a photographer based in New York City. He works on advertising, commercial, editorial and architectural photography.

RICKY'S ENSENADA-STYLE FISH TACOS

RECIPE BY RICKY PIÑA & PHOTOGRAPH BY RYAN DAUSCH
FOOD STYLING BY CHRISTOPHER BARSCH & PROP STYLING BY KIRA CORBIN

When it comes to fish tacos, Ricky Piña is the king. Master of his own taco truck in East Hollywood, Ricky took time out from making people's bellies very happy to share his famous recipe with us. Made in the authentic Ensenada style—the birthplace of fish tacos in Baja, Mexico—Ricky's tacos may be made with lard, but that makes them all the more authentic (and delicious).

FOR THE BEER BATTER	FOR THE FISH AND MARINADE
3 cups (375 grams) all-purpose flour	*5 lean catfish fillets (about 1 1/2–2 pounds)*
1/2 cup (70 grams) dried Mexican oregano	*8 cups (1.9 liters) water*
1/2 cup (115 grams) yellow American mustard	*1/2 cup (115 grams) garlic powder*
1 tablespoon (15 milliliters) vegetable oil	*2 tablespoons (30 grams) salt*
1 teaspoon (5 grams) salt	*2 quarts (1.6 kilograms) lard or vegetable oil*
10 to 14 ounces (295–415 milliliters) Tecate beer, or another Mexican beer	*1 cup (125 grams) all-purpose flour, for coating*

METHOD For the beer batter: Mix all of the ingredients until the mixture has the consistency of pancake batter. Start with less beer and add more if needed. The batter should be thick enough to coat the fish, but not so thick that it sticks on the fish. Set the batter in the refrigerator while you make the marinade.

For the fish and marinade: Cut fillets diagonally into 1-inch-wide by 3-inch-long pieces. In a large bowl, mix the water with the garlic powder and salt. Add the fillets to the seasoned water. Let the fish marinate in the refrigerator for 1 to 2 hours.

When ready, take the batter and fish out of the refrigerator. Drain the fish from the marinade and pat dry. In a large frying pan, add enough lard or vegetable oil to fill the pan 3 inches deep. There should be enough fat in the pan to allow the fish to float. Heat the lard or vegetable oil to 350°F (177°C).

Put the flour in a shallow bowl or plate and dip each piece of fish in the flour to coat, shaking off the excess. Then dip in the batter. Using tongs, carefully add the coated fish to the hot oil, working in batches. Cook on one side for about 2 to 3 minutes until it starts to float, then turn each fillet over and cook until they are golden brown on all sides.

TOPPINGS Pico de gallo: Mix together 5 diced tomatoes, half a chopped onion, 1 to 2 seeded and diced jalapeños, chopped cilantro and lime juice. Season with salt to taste.

Crème: Mix together 1 cup mayonnaise, 1 tablespoon sour cream, 1 pinch salt, 1 tablespoon yellow mustard and 1/3 cup of milk. Chill until ready to use.

Very finely shred half of a medium-size green cabbage.

ASSEMBLY Warm some corn or flour tortillas. Add one strip of fried fish. Top with cabbage first, then add pico de gallo and finish with a drizzle of crème. ○ ○ ○

Serves 8

KING OF THE CASTLE

Professional sandcastle architect Rusty Croft offers some pointers on how to craft the perfect castle.

WORDS BY GEORGIA FRANCES KING &
ILLUSTRATIONS BY SARAH BURWASH

P rofessional sandcastle builder doesn't sound like a bad career choice, does it? Rusty Croft's first paid sandcastle gig was in 1997 when he helped build a 70-foot sculpture in San Diego. Since then he's won several international titles and can count himself as one of the best builders in the world. He tells us a little about competitive castle-ing.

ARE ALL SANDS CREATED EQUAL?

Building a sand sculpture is simple, but it isn't easy. Surprisingly, our most detailed super-cool work is not made with beach sand. Our favorite sand comes from a quarry—it's sharp and hasn't been tumbled by wind and water for eons. It's the difference between stacking cubes and stacking marbles. A beach with heavy wave action is going to have horrible sand, but one that's around the corner from a jetty or in a harbor usually has great sand.

WHAT ARE YOUR FAVORITE PARTS OF THE SIMPLICITY OF SAND AS A MEDIUM?

There's the social aspect: You can't go to the beach, build a sand sculpture and be a jerk or spend the day alone. Sand is a great icebreaker and a wonderful way to keep that sense of childlike wonder. You're engaging adults who probably haven't thought about anything like this in a long time.

YOUR KIDS MUST THINK YOU'RE THE COOLEST DAD IN THE WORLD.

My daughters think everyone does this. I'm always pretty perplexed when they ask kids, "Your dad *doesn't* build giant sand sculptures?"

WERE YOU A SANDCASTLE BUILDER WHEN YOU WERE YOUNGER?

More of a mud pie guy, because I'm from Iowa.

WHAT'S THE WORLD OF COMPETITIVE SANDCASTLE BUILDING LIKE?

Contests have moved away from individual prize money and toward the show-up fee. This is what we do for a living. We're not weekend warriors. We need to be paid! You should take it seriously but not get too invested in something that'll be ultimately judged by someone else. It's art.

WHAT ARE THE BASIC CONSTRUCTION TOOLS?

Bring a sprayer to keep the structure wet, buckets for hauling water and silverware is fantastic for carving and decoration (stainless steel won't rust). But the tool to take it to the professional level is a straw. I wear one on a lanyard around my neck. You can use it to blow the sand crumbs out of cracks. It's a pneumatic particle accelerator and a sand sculptor's best friend.

HOW DO YOU CREATE THE STRONGEST FOUNDATION?

First shovel up a little base pile. Make a hole in the top and pour the water in so it looks like a volcano. Let the water soak in and then pat the whole thing down. Next, use a bucket that has the bottom cut out and put it on top with the wide end down. Fill it with half sand and half water, then shake. Bubbles will rise up. While there's still water in the bucket, throw in more sand and repeat until the compacted sand reaches the top. Take off the bucket and you're ready to start.

WHAT'S THE BEST SAND-TO-WATER RATIO?

There are three keys to a good sand sculpture: water, water and more water. You want to *drench* it. If you have trouble, stop everything and pour water on it. Absolutely too much is just enough.

WHAT MISTAKES DO PEOPLE OFTEN MAKE?

After you've made your structure, start at the top and work your way down with your carving and decoration: If you don't, then you're going to bury your own work in sand. Detail, finish, move down.

WHAT LESSONS HAVE YOU LEARNED THAT CAN BE APPLIED TO DAILY LIFE?

It's about letting go and creating for the moment. A lot of people ask, "Aren't you just devastated to see them wrecked?" But I never am. Sand is a practically free material so you can mess up and it's no big deal. It's not like messing up a $40,000 chunk of marble. To a fly that only lives 24 hours, my sand sculpture lasts a week, and that might as well be eternity. It teaches you about impermanence and how to be extremely flexible. ○ ○ ○

A WHITER SHADE OF PALE

WORDS BY GAIL O'HARA & PHOTOGRAPH BY MARCUS MØLLER BITSCH

No matter where your skin tone falls on the pigment spectrum,
you really should get out in the sun, at least for short bursts. But for those
who are lobster-prone, there are ways to survive the sun and the burn.

A tan is a wonderful thing to have—if you can get a tan. Although we cannot advocate tanning beds, spray tan or orange face and body paint, attempts at tanning naturally can end up hurting, burning and peeling those with a ghostly pallor. If you have a naturally darker complexion, you may be safer from sunburn, but you should still take care to keep your skin healthy and hydrated. And getting some sun can mean more than just a healthy glow: Sunshine is the best way to get vitamin D, which helps your body absorb healthy levels of calcium and phosphorus, improves bone health and may also keep osteoporosis, high blood pressure, cancer and other diseases away.

So how much sun is enough and how much is too much? Here in the Pacific Northwest, public health officials suggest soaking it up for 20 to 30 minutes a day between May and October—sans sunscreen—in order to store it up for the rest of the year. If you fancy getting a bit of color but want to avoid third-degree burns, we've put together a guide for you to prepare your body for the burning sun before, during and after the blaze.

EAT TONS OF SALSA (OR BRUSCHETTA OR SPAGHETTI) A study published in the *British Journal of Dermatology* suggests that eating lots of lycopene-containing tomatoes (most highly concentrated in the cooked variety) resulted in a higher tolerance to ultraviolet light exposure.

INGEST AN AWFUL LOT OF CHOCOLATE A German study revealed that inhaling lots of chocolate led to a 25 percent decrease in skin reddening and potentially fights skin cancer (as if we needed an excuse!).

PUT BROCCOLI ON YOUR FACE Researchers at the University of Arizona also found that putting pureed broc in face cream helps slow burning. Eating fruit and veggies prepares the skin for a scorching day out.

DUCK AND COVER Get decked out in massive sunglasses, enormous hats and sun-proof clothing. Set up camp beneath a grand old tree or an oversize umbrella.

MAKE YOUR OWN SUNSCREEN Recent studies have revealed that many sunscreens and products containing SPF protection also contain carcinogenic ingredients and may be more dangerous to your body than actual sunburn. Use a search engine to discover some easy recipes for making your own homemade sunblock or check the Environmental Working Group's list of less harmful brands.

PLANT AN ALOE GARDEN Known as the "plant of immortality," aloe vera is a magical burn healer and the most soothing thing on a severe sunburn. Its use can be traced back 6,000 years to Egypt.

TAKE DRUGS The Mayo Clinic recommends taking an anti-inflammatory, applying a cold compress and using moisturizing or hydrocortisone cream to feel less pain post-burn.

STAY INSIDE If you can't stand the sun, you could always become a goth or a recluse. In some places, staying indoors in the air-conditioning may be the best way to spend the summer. ○ ○ ○

Gail O'Hara isn't a goth but she's always had the skin tone of one. Formerly an editor at Time Out New York, ELLEgirl *and* SPIN, *she is the managing editor of* Kinfolk *and the publisher of* chickfactor.

HIGH-RISE HARVEST

WORDS BY KELSEY VALA & PHOTOGRAPH BY WILLIAM HEREFORD

Rooftop salt harvesting may seem like an incredulous idea, but in New York anything that can be imagined can be crafted. We asked Sarah Sproule from Urban Sproule a few questions about evaporating sea salt 17 stories above Manhattan.

WHEN DID YOU FIRST HAVE THE IDEA TO HARVEST SEA SALT IN AN URBAN ENVIRONMENT?

I remember the exact moment: I was demo cooking at Union Square Greenmarket using ingredients from regional farms and farmers. I started to season the meal with salt from who-knows-where and it dawned on me that I must make a salt I know about. I thought about all the beekeepers and the hydroponic greenhouses on warehouse rooftops in Brooklyn and Queens, and I thought that if they can do it, why can't I? I didn't set out to make salt on a rooftop in Midtown, but one crystal led to another and here we are.

WHAT DID YOU DO BEFORE YOU STARTED URBAN SPROULE?

I went to school at Le Cordon Bleu, then moved to California to cook at a small farm-to-table restaurant in Palm Springs. After working as chef de cuisine at a steakhouse, I briefly worked in Tucson, Arizona, for James Beard Award–winning chef Janos Wilder before moving to New York in 2011.

HOW WERE YOU LOGISTICALLY ABLE TO BUILD A SALT HOUSE IN MIDTOWN MANHATTAN?

The salt farm is located in the north end of Chelsea, an interesting part of town right on the cusp of Hell's Kitchen. I started in the summer of 2012 on a rooftop of a music school with four small rolling salt houses about 4 feet tall, which produced about 15 pounds of salt that fall. I quickly decided to expand and now have an 8-by-12-foot greenhouse. Operating in the city is fun but challenging: Lumber for building a greenhouse is hard to come by in the middle of Manhattan, not to mention heavy and cumbersome! And we've luckily never had a problem with pigeons.

HOW DID YOU CHOOSE THE BODY OF WATER YOU'D COLLECT YOUR SEAWATER FROM, AND HOW DOES THIS AFFECT THE FLAVOR PROFILE OF THE SALT?

Salt has a *terroir,* if you will. What affects the taste of salt is directly related to where your salt called home. After making a lot of salt from different areas around Long Island, I decided I wanted seawater, straight up. I contacted the fishermen at American Pride Seafood, a local Long Island fishery known for its outstandingly fresh seafood, and thought that if their fish tastes better than everyone else's, then it's got to be the water out there. They enthusiastically agreed to bring me seawater and it was born: sea salt made from water 30 miles east off the coast of Montauk. We're the only salt makers in the world that harvest water from so far offshore in EPA-approved waters, so the level of purity is unmatched.

HOW HAVE YOU FELT THE SALT TRADE HAS CHANGED IN THE PAST FEW CENTURIES?

It's a trade that, up until 150 years ago, was not a monopolized industry. In the 1700s, entire towns in Cape Cod would have salt field harvest days and all the residents would participate. It was a community effort because everyone needed the salt. People don't know how salt is made and reintroducing the process is one of the most enjoyable parts of this job. ○ ○ ○

For more information about Sarah's salts, visit urbansproule.com.

A CULINARY SALT ROUNDTABLE

The past decade has seen something of a revolution among the small-batch salt industry. We asked a variety of chefs, food writers, salt harvesters and experts to answer a few questions about how, why and when to use salt.

PHOTOGRAPH BY ANJA VERDUGO

MICHAEL ANTHONY: executive chef/partner, Gramercy Tavern (New York, New York)

ASHLEY RODRIGUEZ: editor, notwithoutsalt.com (Seattle, Washington)

BEN JACOBSEN: founder, Jacobsen Salt Co. (Portland and Netarts, Oregon)

SARAH SPROULE: salt maker/owner, Urban Sproule (New York, New York)

MARK KURLANSKY: author of *Salt: A World History* (New York, New York)

JENN LOUIS: chef/owner, Lincoln and Sunshine Tavern (Portland, Oregon)

VITALY PALEY: chef/owner, Paley's Place, Imperial and Portland Penny Diner (Portland, Oregon)

TODD KNOLL: executive chef, Jordan Vineyard & Winery (Healdsburg, California)

LISA FAIN: author of *The Homesick Texan's Family Table* (New York, New York)

BRYANT TERRY: chef and author of *Afro-Vegan* and *Vegan Soul Kitchen* (Oakland, California)

HOW HAVE YOU SEEN PEOPLE'S SALT HABITS CHANGE OVER TIME?

Lisa: When I was young, it seemed there was only one kind of salt available: iodized table salt. These days most people will have at least two kinds of salt in their pantries, and even if they don't they're a lot more aware that there are many different kinds of salt available.

Bryant: My parents only cook with sea salt nowadays, which is a big leap for them.

Ashley: I'm not sure if I've noticed habits change, but I'm glad salt's poor reputation is being redeemed. When you're cooking food from real ingredients in your home, there's no need to fear the overuse of salt. People understand that and have learned to not be afraid of it.

Todd: I honestly don't believe that practices have seen much change. While we're more conscious of sodium's effect on health, seasoning habits are formed early.

Vitaly: I know I've changed my own perception of salt. We spend so much time sourcing the best products but then add the most common industrialized salt to season them. It makes no sense.

Sarah: Back in the Middle Ages, spoiled meat would be doused in salt and spices to hide the rancid odor and taste, making it practically inedible by modern-day standards. Now we see convenience food companies using salts in the same manner by loading their chips and crackers with enough salt to make them shelf-stable for years. People are concerned about salt intake—I like to call it the "sodium craze." But health conditions related to sodium intake haven't come out of garnishing with your favorite artisanal flake salt: They've come from consuming packaged foods loaded with overly processed sodium.

HOW DOES THE ORIGIN OF A PARTICULAR SALT AFFECT THE FLAVOR?

Ben: Salt tastes different no matter where it comes from. I tested more than 25 spots along the Oregon and Washington coasts to come up with our location. The quality varies depending on the location, much like grape qualities vary from place to place. A wine grape is different if it comes from a hot, sunny hillside than when it comes from a cool, shady valley. The same is true with water and where it comes from. Water from a shallow, calm bay with few inputs varies greatly from water in a turbid ocean with plenty of direct freshwater inflows.

Ashley: Like *terroir* in wine, the flavor of salt is affected by where it's harvested. Perhaps that's why I'm partial to the San Juan salts as I've grown up splashing in its waves, so it tastes familiar to me. Or maybe that's all in my head. Either way I like that romantic notion, so I'll go with it.

Todd: This is what makes it fun and interesting. Some collection points may be from somewhat brackish waters that result in great minerality and a pleasing irregularity and crunch, or there may be seaweed present in the pools at the tide's edge that bring out iodine notes and a natural affinity for seafood. For purity, I look to northern Japan and Europe.

Lisa: A salt's origin does affect its flavor. Hawaiian red salt is earthier and less bright than Himalayan pink salt. And Pacific Ocean salt seems brinier than Galveston Bay salt. Though all salts, whatever their origin, make food taste better.

DO YOU HAVE ANY SALT-RELATED MEMORIES FROM YOUR CAREER OR CHILDHOOD?

Ashley: I remember my mom encouraging me to put a pinch of salt on a slice of a Granny Smith apple. We were sitting at the counter and I noticed her dusting her slice with fine salt. At first I thought she was mad until I tried a taste and couldn't believe that the apple actually tasted sweeter. It has stayed with me all these years.

Vitaly: Salt played a big part of preserving things when I was growing up in Russia. I used to watch my grandfather make salted herring, sauerkraut and pickles every year in the fall.

Todd: Having been raised in Hawaii, salt was an important part of my childhood. We'd dive for fish in the morning and season our catch with cheap soy sauce or salt collected in the tide pools.

Bryant: I used to love eating watermelon with salt sprinkled on it during the height of summer on my grandmother's porch in Memphis. That's the proper way to eat watermelon in the South.

Lisa: My family likes to tell a story about my aunt and her first batch of ice cream. When she first married my uncle, she didn't have much experience in the kitchen but was eager to learn, and one hot day she decided it would be fun to surprise everyone with homemade ice cream. She'd never made it before but she found a recipe and got to work. Well, this was back in the old days when you needed rock salt to keep the canister chilled as you churned the cream. However, my aunt misread the recipe and thought the rock salt belonged in the custard, not in the ice cream maker. Needless to say, the ice cream ended up inedible.

WHAT'S YOUR FAVORITE WAY TO USE SALT?

Jenn: Always top chocolate chip cookies with sea salt halfway through baking them or put flaky sea salt on top of chocolate ice cream. Salt on sweets is awesome.

Ben: Slice a great baguette. Spread with good butter. Sprinkle with Jacobsen Flake Salt. It's incredibly simple and just so good.

Vitaly: Salt-curing foie gras.

Lisa: I throw a bit of salt into my morning banana smoothie and it not only enhances the fruit's flavor but also makes it seem even sweeter. Salt can be magical that way.

ANY ODD USES OF SALT THAT YOU CAN RECOMMEND?

Sarah: If you make a pot of coffee and let it sit on the heat for too long, making it bitter, try adding a pinch of salt to your coffee cup before you throw out the brew.

Mark: I have the habit of dressing salad with nothing but olive oil and coarse salt. This was a misunderstanding of what the Romans did (they used brine) but by the time I realized my mistake, I was already hooked.

Ashley: Salt is in my oatmeal, on top of my cookies, in my hot chocolate and even beside me while I paint. I love the texture it gives to watercolors.

Todd: We roast all of our root vegetables in coarse sea salt. Cover unpeeled beets in it and roast until they're easily pierced by a paring knife—they'll be unmatched in color and flavor concentration.

Bryant: I toss cabbage with salt before making coleslaw. The cabbage wilts and releases excess liquid so the slaw isn't too watery.

DO YOU COOK WITH LESS SALT AS YOU EXPECT YOUR DINERS TO ADD SALT AUTOMATICALLY?

Michael: No, we season food with a particular style in mind, searching for full flavor without overdoing it. But we do offer salt at every table for two reasons: It's anticipating a guest request, and it's interactive and fun for people to use.

Vitaly: We season food the way it's intended to be eaten. We don't have saltshakers at the table and only provide salt on request.

Ben: Yes, I always have a couple of cellars of salt on my table for people to finish their food on their own. You end up eating less salt than if the food was pre-seasoned, and it just tastes better.

Lisa: I cook with as much salt as I feel a dish needs. Although, I'm annoyed when I'm at a restaurant and there isn't any salt available on the table. People's preferences are different, and if you want to add more salt to a dish, then you should be able to.

Bryant: If it's a cooked dish, I believe that the chef did not do his or her job well if diners have to add salt at the table (save for a sprinkle of finishing salt for added zing).

Ashley: It's important to note that salt shouldn't just be saved till the end of the cooking process and that it's important to salt throughout. I throw a pinch in as my onions slowly soften in butter and then again when I add in the rest of the vegetables. This way everything is being seasoned. If you save the salting until the end, then the food will be flat and just taste of salt.

DO YOU HARVEST YOUR OWN SALT?

Ben: We harvest our salt from Netarts Bay, Oregon. It's taken me three years to figure out how to make our salt and it's the best in the world. It has the perfect delicate crunch and tastes briny but not bitter or astringent. It's a very deliberate taste and texture profile.

Sarah: I collect the water, filter, evaporate and harvest inside my Manhattan rooftop greenhouse called a salt house. I befriended Charlie and Glenn from American Pride Seafood, who gather the purest seawater for me when they're out fishing 30 miles east of Montauk.

Todd: Collecting salts has been a part of our travels for years now. It's the perfect souvenir as each salt has a distinct place and time. What better way to celebrate an anniversary than with a romantic meal finished with the salt collected during a honeymoon? My wife and I have collected salts from locations in Hawaii, the Greek islands, Monterey, Baja and Cozumel.

Ashley: My oldest son and I started our own little salt business a few years ago. We'd go to the beach, fill a couple of milk jugs, splash around in the seawater for a while then head home to filter and start boiling. I loved the excuse to head to the beach and get my feet wet. We packaged the salt in little glass tubes and labeled them with stickers that read "sea salt" with a skull and crossbones in the middle—not because the salt was toxic, but because he was really into pirates then. Then I went to a book signing with Mark Bitterman. I proudly had him taste the salt my five-year-old and I made and he raved about it. ○ ○ ○

THE SALT AND VINEGAR MENU (CONTINUED FROM PAGE 37)

SHAVED SUMMER SQUASH SALAD WITH CHARRED CORN

RECIPE BY DIANA YEN & THE JEWELS OF NEW YORK

Colorful summer squash makes for a wonderfully light side dish when shaved raw into ribbons. The entire squash can be eaten with its skin, seeds and all. This refreshing salad is topped with baby heirloom tomatoes, charred corn and fresh ricotta.

1 ear corn, shucked

Canola oil, for brushing

1/4 cup (25 grams) finely minced shallot

1 garlic clove, minced

1/4 cup (60 milliliters) apple cider vinegar

1 tablespoon (15 grams) Dijon mustard

1 tablespoon (20 grams) honey

1/2 cup (120 milliliters) extra-virgin olive oil

4 medium-size summer squashes (a mix of zucchini and yellow squashes), thinly shaved on a mandolin

1 1/2 cups (230 grams) baby heirloom tomatoes, cut in half crosswise

1/2 cup (115 grams) fresh ricotta

1/4 cup (10 grams) fresh basil leaves, torn

Salt and pepper to taste

METHOD Preheat the grill to medium-high heat. Rub the corn ear with canola oil and season with salt and pepper. Grill, turning as needed, until evenly browned and tender, about 15–20 minutes. Let it cool and then slice the corn off the cob in thick strips. Set aside.

Meanwhile, combine the shallot, garlic and vinegar in a medium bowl. Add the Dijon mustard and honey, and slowly whisk in the olive oil until the dressing binds. Season with salt and pepper to taste.

Combine half of the vinaigrette with the summer squash, tomatoes and corn. Toss and let sit for 5 minutes. Serve on a large platter and garnish with the ricotta and basil. Drizzle with the remainder of the dressing. ○ ○ ○

Serves 6

SPECIAL THANKS
Paintings Katie Stratton

ON THE COVER
Photograph Charlie Schuck
Models Jennae Quisenberry at Heffner Management
Eric Winsterly at TCM Models
Studio Director Shandrea Gilchrist
Digital Imaging Manager Alex Nekrasov

WRITING THE WAVES, A LETTER FROM PEPPER
AND THE CASE FOR CRYING
Photographer's Assistants Laura Jennings and Chris Low
Handwriting Michelle Cho
Special thanks to Sandbox Studios and Roster Reps

SALT AND VINEGAR MENU
Special thanks to Pat Bates and Associates

THE LINGERING SALT OF SWEAT
Photographer's Assistant Lauren Colton
Assistant Stylist Margaret Jones
Hair & Makeup Kaija Towner

Clothing:
Tie-dye jumpsuit, *Black Crane*
Romper, *Chimala*
White blouse, *Apiece Apart*
White T-shirt, *R13*
Straw hat, *stylist's own*
All available at Totokaelo.com (except hat)

SULTAN OF SALT
Special thanks to Kaitlin Hansen & the Meadow

BREAKING THE ICE: A SNOW CONE PRIMER
Special thanks to Little Freshie

THE SALT FLATS OF BOLIVIA
Images © Scarlett Hooft Graafland,
Courtesy Michael Hoppen Contemporary

LIFE ON THE WATER
Production Helle Walsted

A GUIDE TO FLIPPING
Production Darling Creative
Divers Georgia Ward, Jing Leung and
Rosie Cardoe at Sports Promotions
Special thanks to Crystal Palace Dive Center

PERU'S SALTED PONDS
Special thanks to Art + Rep

RICKY'S ENSENADA-STYLE FISH TACOS
Follow Ricky on Twitter to find his tacos: @RickysFishTacos

KING OF THE CASTLE
For more information, visit sandguys.com

SUBSCRIBE

VISIT WWW.KINFOLK.COM/SHOP
FOUR ISSUES EACH YEAR

CONTACT US
If you have questions or comments,
contact us at *info@kinfolk.com*

SUBSCRIPTIONS
For questions about your subscription,
email us at *subscribe@kinfolk.com*

STOCKISTS
If you'd like to carry *Kinfolk*,
get in touch at *distribution@kinfolk.com*

SUBMISSIONS
To pitch a story, write us at
submissions@kinfolk.com

WWW.KINFOLK.COM

KEEP IN TOUCH